# RAGING RIVERS

## ANITA GANERI

Illustrated by
Mike Phillips

Hippo

**Also available:**
*Violent Volcanoes*
*Odious Oceans*
*Stormy Weather*

**Coming soon in this series:**
*Desperate Deserts*
*Earth-shattering Earthquakes*

Scholastic Children's Books,
Commonwealth House, 1–19 New Oxford Street,
London WC1A 1NU, UK

A division of Scholastic Ltd
London ~ New York ~ Toronto ~ Sydney ~ Auckland
Mexico City ~ New Delhi ~ Hong Kong

First published in the UK by Scholastic Ltd, 2000

Text copyright © Anita Ganeri, 2000
Illustrations copyright © Mike Phillips, 2000

ISBN 0 439 01363 1

All rights reserved
Typeset by M Rules
Printed and bound by Nørhaven Paperback, Viborg, Denmark

10 9

# CONTENTS

# INTRODUCTION

Geography is full of horrible surprises. Take learning about rotten rivers, for a start. One minute, you're sitting in your nice, warm classroom, nodding happily off to sleep while your geography teacher's voice goes on and on and on. . .

TODAY'S LESSON IS ALL ABOUT FLUVIAL BEDLOADS.* OPEN YOUR BOOKS AT PAGE BLAH, BLAH, BLAH...

* That's the tricky technical term for a river's sandy bottom.

You close your eyes and start to dream. . . You're sitting on a grassy riverbank, a long, cold drink in one hand, a fishing rod in the other. Lovely. The sun is shining, the birds are singing, geography doesn't seem so boring after all. Bliss.

Suddenly, your dream turns nasty. Really nasty. Now you're standing in the pouring rain, up to your knees in muddy

5

water. Feeling like a drowned rat. What a nightmare. Yes, your teacher's taken you on a ghastly geography field trip. And it's HORRIBLE.

So horrible that you're glad to wake up and find yourself back in your geography lesson again. It may be boring but at least it's dry.

...BLAH, BLAH, BLAHDY, BLAH...

But not all geography is dismally damp and uncomfortable. Some bits are horribly exciting and interesting. Try this simple experiment. Smile sweetly at your mum, dad or guardian and tell them you're off for a bath. Don't wait for a reply, they'll be too shocked to speak. Go into the bathroom and turn the taps on full. How long does it take the bath to fill up? About ten minutes? Now try to imagine 200 MILLION bath taps turned on full. This is how much water it takes to fill the awesome Amazon, the biggest river on Earth. (Back in your bathroom, pull out the plug, flap your towel around, and pretend you've had a good, long soak. Your grown-up will be ever so impressed.)

And that's what this book is all about. Long enough to stretch right around the world, strong enough to carve out mile-deep valleys, angry enough to flood a whole town, with wicked waterfalls as tall as the Eiffel Tower, rushing rivers are all the rage. In *Raging Rivers*, you can. . .

- explore the world's greatest rivers with Travis, your intrepid tour guide.

- take the plunge over the world's highest waterfalls.

- catch and cook a piranha for lunch (mind your fingers).

• learn how to survive in a flood (against all the odds).

This is geography like never before. And it certainly isn't boring. All you have to do is keep turning the pages. You don't even need to get wet. Unless, of course, you drop your book in the bath. . .

## The amazing adventures of Lewis and Clark
## Washington DC, USA, 1803

The two young men summoned to President Thomas Jefferson's office shivered slightly, although the room was warm. They had just been handed the most important mission of their lives – to lead the first ever official expedition across the wild west of America to find a river route to the Pacific Ocean.

Jefferson's idea was to open up these lands for trade and settlement, and to make America richer and more powerful than ever before. There was just one problem. No one had explored these vast lands before. No one knew what dangers lay ahead for them or if they would ever make it back home. It was enough to make anyone shiver. President Jefferson shook their hands and wished them goodbye and good luck. He didn't care what other people said. He was sure that he'd found the right men for the job.

The two men in question were dashing Captain Meriwether Lewis, the President's trusty private secretary, and Lewis's old friend, Lieutenant William Clark. They were young, strong, brave and handsome. They'd need to be all of these things (OK, so good looks weren't that important). It was going to be a long and rocky road. Lewis and Clark put their heads together and soon they'd hatched a daring plan. They would travel up the Missouri River, as far as they could go, cross the Rocky Mountains, then follow the Columbia River to the Pacific. Simple!

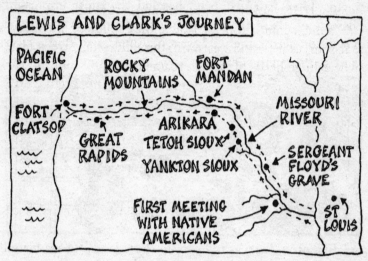

They spent the winter preparing for the expedition. They were not travelling alone. With them went a group of 43 men, mostly soldiers, grandly named the Corps of Discovery. They also took six tonnes of food (when this ran out, they'd have to hunt for more), weapons, medicines, scientific equipment and gifts for the local people.

These were loaded into three sturdy boats – one barge and two canoes. These were crucial. Without good boats, it was sink or swim.

At last, on Monday 14 May, 1804, everything was ready. A single shot was fired to signal the off and the expedition headed out of the town of St Louis on the banks of the Missouri. It would be two and a half years before they would see home again. From St Louis, they followed the mighty Missouri as it wound westward, through rolling green plains where huge herds of buffalo roamed. For five months, they made steady progress. Canoeing upriver, watching the world go by, was really quite pleasant. The only flies in the ointment were the swarms of mosquitoes constantly buzzing around their heads. Very irritating.

In October, they reached the land of the Mandan Indians. They were warmly welcomed, and decided to spend the winter there because the river would soon be covered in ice.

The winter of 1804–1805 was very long, very cold and very boring. On some days, temperatures plummeted to a teeth-chattering low of -40°C. The members of the expedition stayed snug and warm (but bored stiff) inside their log cabins. It was far, far too cold to risk setting foot outside those four walls.

By the following April, they were all glad to be on the move again. There was just one tiny hitch. So far, they'd been able to follow their route on some roughly-drawn charts but from here on the maps ran out. Completely. What lay ahead was utterly unknown territory. Without maps, Lewis and Clark had no idea what they were in for – whether or not they'd be hiking up mountains, wading through rivers or hacking their way through vegetation. There was just no knowing. And they could only hope that they were going in the right direction!

But plucky Lewis and Clark weren't worried. They hired a local Indian guide to help them out – someone who did know the lay of the land – and continued upriver to the Rocky Mountains. Now came the worst part of the journey. Crossing the mountains was a terrible ordeal. Their food ran short and at night the weather turned bitterly cold. All the men could do was grit their chattering teeth and keep plodding grimly on.

Their courage paid off. On the other side of the mountains lay wide open plains . . . and the Columbia River. Finally, on 7 November 1805, they sailed down the river to its mouth in the sea. At last, they had reached the Pacific Ocean and their journey's end.

The following spring, they began their long journey home again, reaching St Louis on 23 September 1806. Lewis and Clark were given a hero's welcome. Everyone was glad to see them, especially as they'd been given up for dead. They'd covered some 7,000 kilometres, most of it by canoe. They'd been growled at by grizzly bears, rattled at by rattlesnakes, and riddled with frostbite, fear and starvation. Lewis had even been shot in the leg by someone who mistook him for a deer! It's true! Despite this, only one man in the team had died, probably from appendicitis. The expedition had been a raging triumph. True, their river route was not very practical. If you weren't a brave explorer, it was much too long and dangerous. (Many Americans did later follow in Lewis and Clark's footsteps, in search of new lands and trade, but they sensibly went overland by wagon.) Geographically, though, it was all a rip-roaring success. Lewis and Clark's expedition journals were crammed full of maps, sketches and notes about the rivers they'd sailed down and the people they'd met. (They kept notes about absolutely everything. That's the sort of thing geographers do.) Places and people that horrible geographers had never seen before.

# GOING WITH THE FLOW

Of course, good old Lewis and Clark weren't the first people to realize just how horribly handy rivers can be. They used rivers to get them from A to B. But people have also been drinking them, washing in them, fishing in them and generally messing about in them for years and years.

The Romans even built a city on one. According to legend, the city of Rome was built by two brothers called Romulus and Remus. They were identical twins. Their mum was the priestess Rhea Silvia. Their dad was Mars, the god of war. So far, so good. The one bad apple in their happy family was their wicked great-uncle, cranky King Amulius.

* That's Roman for cheese.

Great-uncle Amulius was worried sick that one day when the twins were older they'd try to seize his throne. So he shoved them in a basket and chucked them into the raging River Tiber. As well as saving his royal skin, it would save him a fortune in birthday presents.

BYE, BYE, BOYS, HEE! HEE! HEE!

The twins drifted downstream and came to a stop at the bottom of the Palatine Hill. There a she-wolf found them. But instead of wolfing them down for lunch, she took them home and brought them up to be nice, well-behaved, er, wolves.

AND I THOUGHT OUR TABLE MANNERS WERE BAD!

Later, they moved in with a kindly shepherd. (They had to promise not to chase the sheep.) But they never forgot their happy wolfhoods and decided to build their old wolf-mum a splendid city on the spot where she'd found them. For her retirement.

Building began. But things soon went horribly wrong. Romulus and Remus fell out big-time, over the height of a wall! You see, Romulus built the wall to defend the city from attack. But Remus said it was useless, way too low to stop anyone. And to prove his point, he jumped over it.

I WISH HE'D GO AND JUMP IN THE RIVER

Romulus was furious. Did the twins make up? Nope, they did not. Romulus pulled out his sword and killed Remus. Then he named the riverbank city after himself.

I NAME THIS CITY... AFTER ME!

So, if you believe your legends, Rome was built next to the River Tiber by a pair of twins brought up by a kindly wolf. Sounds reasonable.

**Teacher teaser**

Outwit your teacher with this Roman river talk:

OOH MISS, LOOK! JENKINS HAS DESCENDED INTO THE FLUVIAL FLOW!

What has Jenkins done?

## What on Earth is a raging river?

Some bits of geography are horribly difficult to understand. Don't worry, you can leave those bits out. This book is about the other bits, the bits that will turn you into a genius geographer without any effort at all. Take raging rivers, for instance. Your teacher may try to bamboozle you with all sorts of boring and baffling facts about rivers. Take no notice. It's just your teacher trying to make himself or herself feel important. Pathetic, eh! The horrible truth is that a river is a stream of freshwater (that means it's not salty like the sea) that flows across the land. Simple!

## Water on the brain

You might think that yummy chocolate milkshake is the most useful and precious liquid on Earth. But you'd be wrong – dead wrong. While you could go for weeks without a milkshake, without water to drink, you'd be dead as a dinosaur in a few days. And where does most of this water come from? From raging rivers, of course. Rivers might only make up one per cent of the Earth's water, but that one per cent is fresh water which, when it's been cleaned, we can drink.

ARE YOU SURE THIS WATER'S BEEN CLEANED?

The first person to study water seriously (well, it takes all sorts) was British scientist, Henry Cavendish (1731-1810). Henry was born in Nice, France but spent most of his life in

London. Now nice Henry was a bit of a loner. He lived with his dad, until his dad died, and didn't go out very much. Well, you wouldn't either if you'd had Henry's dire dress sense. His favourite outfit was a hopelessly unfashionable purple suit, with a frilly collar and matching cuffs, topped off by a threadbare three-cornered hat. It looked frightful. No wonder Henry didn't have many friends. He certainly didn't have a girlfriend. In fact, he wouldn't even allow girls to set foot in his house. He thought they were a bad influence.

Luckily, Henry had one saving grace. He was absolutely brilliant at chemistry. He spent most of his time in his house, doing chaotic chemistry experiments. (He much preferred chemistry to people. After all, test tubes couldn't talk back.)

Anyway, when lucky Henry was 40 years old, he inherited a million pounds. He was rich! But did he let the money go to his head? Oh no. Did he blow all his cash on fine wine, fancy clothes or exotic holidays? Nope, he did not. He continued to work as hard as ever and spent most of his lovely lolly on . . . guess what? You've got it, it went on yet more chemistry kits and chemistry books. And it was just as well for horrible geography that it did because not long afterwards Henry Cavendish made the most amazing discovery. One day, in his laboratory, he mixed up some hydrogen and oxygen gas in a jar and heated the mixture up. What do you think he saw?

ⓐ The sides of the jar covered with soot?

ⓑ The sides of the jar covered with water?

ⓒ The sides of the jar covered with slime?

**Answer: b)** The sides of the jar were covered with water. What brainy Henry had discovered was that water is not made of one single substance (i.e. plain old water) as single-minded scientists thought. In fact, it's made up of two gases, hydrogen and oxygen. The reaction between the two created water vapour which condensed (turned into liquid water) when it touched the sides of the jar. Incredible. In chemists' code, freshwater is called $H_2O$. That means two hydrogen atoms and one oxygen atom joined together as a water molecule. And billions and billions of wonderful water molecules make up a raging river.

Today, someone like Henry might be called a horrible hydrologer. That's the posh name for a geographer who studies river water. And hooray Henry was frightfully posh. Both his grandfathers were frightfully posh dukes who left Henry pots of frightfully posh dosh!

*Earth-shattering fact*
*But where on Earth does all this horrible $H_2O$ come from? It can't all be made in chemistry jars. And how does it get into raging rivers? Here's an Earth-shattering fact for you to flow with. The water found in raging rivers has flowed millions and millions of times before. In the water cycle, it's recycled again and again. So the water flowing in the awesome Amazon may once have flowed through Ancient Rome. Mindboggling, eh? To see how the water cycle works, imagine you're one of hard-working Henry's marvellous molecules. (Better still, imagine your geography teacher as one.) OK, so you'll have to use your imagination!*

*You're about to go on a very long journey. Over the page there's a picture to show you the way. Are you ready to go with the flow?*

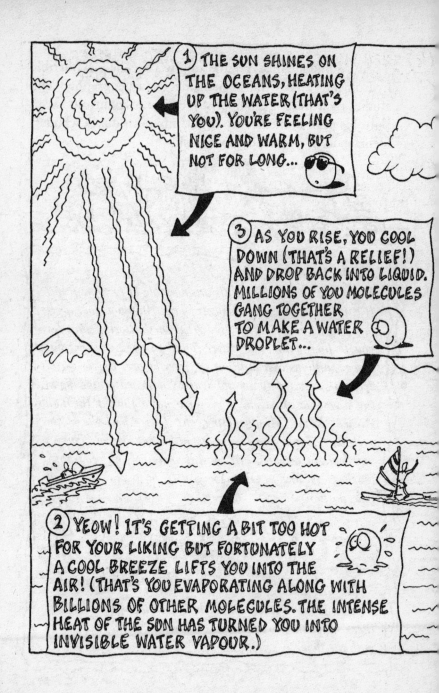

22

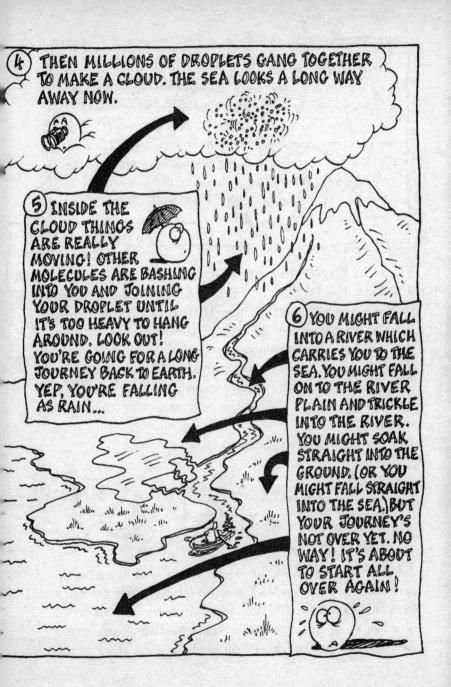

**4** THEN MILLIONS OF DROPLETS GANG TOGETHER TO MAKE A CLOUD. THE SEA LOOKS A LONG WAY AWAY NOW.

**5** INSIDE THE CLOUD THINGS ARE REALLY MOVING! OTHER MOLECULES ARE BASHING INTO YOU AND JOINING YOUR DROPLET UNTIL IT'S TOO HEAVY TO HANG AROUND. LOOK OUT! YOU'RE GOING FOR A LONG JOURNEY BACK TO EARTH. YEP, YOU'RE FALLING AS RAIN...

**6** YOU MIGHT FALL INTO A RIVER WHICH CARRIES YOU TO THE SEA. YOU MIGHT FALL ON TO THE RIVER PLAIN AND TRICKLE INTO THE RIVER. YOU MIGHT SOAK STRAIGHT INTO THE GROUND. (OR YOU MIGHT FALL STRAIGHT INTO THE SEA.) BUT YOUR JOURNEY'S NOT OVER YET. NO WAY! IT'S ABOUT TO START ALL OVER AGAIN!

## How on Earth do rivers flow?

1 Rivers always flow downhill. Which seems horribly obvious when you realize that they're dragged down by gravity. It's the same when you go downhill on your bike. You don't need to pedal – gravity does all the work. Gravity is a force which brings things down to Earth. It's what keeps your feet on the ground. It happens when a large object (the Earth) pulls a small object (the river or you on your bike) towards it.

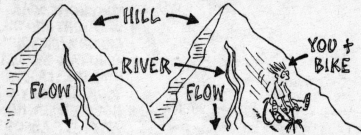

2 A river doesn't always flow at the same speed. It speeds up and slows down. This isn't because the river gets tired, it's because of a force called friction. You get friction when two objects try to push past each other and slow each other down, like when you're out shopping and get stuck in the

crowds. What's this got to do with rivers? Well, sometimes, friction between the river (Object No. 1) and its bed and banks (Object No. 2) slows the water down. A river flows fastest on the surface, near the middle, where friction is much weaker.

## See how fast a river flows

*What you need:*

- a stopwatch
- a tape measure
- two sticks
- an orange
- a river

*What you do:*

a) Measure out a 10-metre stretch of river bank. Mark the start and end with the sticks.

**b)** Drop the orange into the water.

**c)** Time the orange as it flows downstream. (That's the direction the water's flowing in.)

**d)** Now for some boring maths. (You can skip this bit if it's too much like homework.) Remember how some bits of river flow faster than others? To work out an average speed for the whole river, you need to multiply your answer by 0.8. For example, if the orange travels 10 metres in 20 seconds, the flow speed is 0.5 metres per second. If you times this by 0.8, you get an average of 0.4 metres per second. (Experts use average speeds to work out things like how much water the river carries. But that's for another maths lesson!)

**3** Rivers flow fastest down steep slopes, and you don't get much steeper than a waterfall. The Niagara River speeds up to 108 km/h as it plummets over Niagara Falls. That's about 16 times normal walking pace. Time to get your running shoes on!

WOW! A RUSHING, RAGING RIVER!

**4** At any time, there's only enough water in all the world's rivers to keep them flowing for about two weeks. Without fresh supplies, they'd quickly dry up.

**5** The Ancient Greeks had some funny ideas about what gets a river flowing. They knew all about the water cycle and all about rain. (A right bunch of know-alls they were.) But they didn't believe for a single minute that enough rain could fall to fill even one raging river.

They thought that the water must come from the sea, flowing into rivers through underground streams (and somehow losing its salty taste on the way).

**6** In 1674, French lawyer, politician and part-time hydrologist Pierre Perrault measured the amount of rain falling in a year over the land drained by the River Seine.

What did he find? He worked out that there was enough rain to fill the Seine six times over and still have some left over for a quick wash. The clever-clogs Greeks had got it wrong!

**7** Horrible geographers now know that water gets into rivers in four different ways. And they all start with rain. Here's Travis to guide you through them.

Some rain falls straight into the river. Simple!

Some rain falls on the ground. It runs downhill into small streams which flow together to make a river.

Some rain falls to the ground and freezes into glaciers. When the weather warms up, parts of the glaciers start to melt. This starts a stream, you can guess the rest!

ICE

Some rain falls and soaks into the ground. Boringly, it's called groundwater. Some of it flows straight into rivers. And as the rivers flow downstream, some rainwater gushes up as a spring.

UNDER GROUND

**8** Luckily, rivers don't have to rely on groundwater for the whole of their water supply. Just as well. They'd be waiting a very long time. Groundwater flows very slowly. Very slowly indeed. This is what one scientist said about it:

A SNAIL MOVES FASTER THAN GROUNDWATER

BROOM! BROOM!

Another scientist, American John Mann, decided to see if this snaily tale was true. You can try his slimy experiment for yourself.

*What you need:*
- a tape measure
- a stopwatch
- a snail
- plenty of spare time on your hands

*What you do:*
**a)** Take the snail out into your garden.
**b)** Put it down on the path.
**c)** Time how long it takes the snail to trail along for a metre. (If you get bored waiting, cut the distance down.)

FINISH

*What do you think happens:*

**a)** The snail leads you up the garden path?

**b)** The snail moves at a snail's pace, obviously?

**c)** The snail moves faster than go-slow groundwater?

---

**Answer: c)** From his experiment, John Mann worked out that groundwater moves at only $\frac{1}{70}$th of a snail's pace. That's 70 times slower than a slowcoach snail! And who said doing science experiments wasn't boring!

---

# Raging river record breakers: test your teacher

After all this flowing to and fro, you'll need a well-earned rest. Why not veg out on the sofa, put your feet up and leave the hard work to somebody else? Somebody like your geography teacher! Test their hydrological know-how with this quick quiz.

**1** The Nile is the longest river on Earth. TRUE/FALSE?

**2** The Amazon holds the most water. TRUE/FALSE?

**3** The shortest river is D River. TRUE/FALSE?

**4** The Rhine is the longest river in Europe. TRUE/FALSE?

**5** Some rivers are usually dry. TRUE/FALSE?

**6** Some rivers are completely frozen in winter. TRUE/FALSE?

---

**Answers:**

**1** TRUE. The record-breaking Nile in Egypt is 6,695 kilometres long, making it officially the world's longest river. But it's a very close thing. The Amazon in South America is just 255 kilometres behind. Some horrible geographers see things differently. According to their measurements, the Amazon comes out longer. (Note: don't worry about these differences. Geographers are always falling out. You see, geography isn't an exact science, which means nobody knows anything for certain. So although geographers like to think they have an answer for everything, it isn't always the same answer!)

**2 TRUE.** The awesome Amazon carries more water than any other river on Earth, 60 times more than the Nile and one fifth of all river water on Earth. At its mouth, the Amazon empties 95,000 litres of water into the sea. EVERY SINGLE MINUTE! That's like emptying out 53 Olympic-sized swimming pools. Compared to this raging river, the Nile's a mere trickle.

**3 TRUE AND FALSE.** It's true that, at just 37 metres long, D River in Oregon, USA, is the world's shortest river. It flows from Devil's Lake into the Pacific Ocean.

**4** FALSE. The vulgar Volga in Russia is 3,530 kilometres long and the longest river in Europe. The Rhine is only 1,320 kilometres long, less than half the Volga's length.

**5** TRUE. Many desert rivers hardly ever have any water in them. Because there's so little rain in the desert, they're dry for much of the year. Other rivers are wet in winter and dry in summer.

**6** TRUE. Every winter, the Ob-Irtysh River in snow-bound Siberia freezes along its whole length. The upper part of the river, high up in the mountains, stays frozen solid for five whole months. Brrr!

*What your teacher's score means. . .*

Allow two points for each correct answer. And no cheating. . .

**10-12 points**. Excellent. With such in-depth knowledge, your teacher will make a top hydrologist.

**6-8 points**. Not bad but the answers aren't quite flowing yet. If your teacher paid a bit more attention in class, he/she might just stay on course.

**4 points and below**. Oh dear! I'm sorry to say but your teacher's far too wet for this type of work. Better stick to teaching. . .

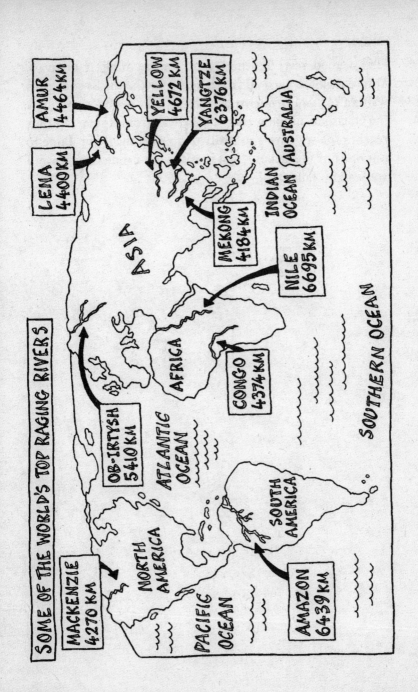

SOME OF THE WORLD'S TOP RAGING RIVERS

AMUR 4464 KM

LENA 4400 KM

YELLOW 4672 KM

YANGTZE 6376 KM

ASIA

MEKONG 4184 KM

NILE 6695 KM

AUSTRALIA

INDIAN OCEAN

OB-IRTYSH 5410 KM

AFRICA

ATLANTIC OCEAN

CONGO 4374 KM

MACKENZIE 4270 KM

NORTH AMERICA

PACIFIC OCEAN

SOUTH AMERICA

AMAZON 6439 KM

SOUTHERN OCEAN

Had a good rest? Feeling ready for anything? I hope so. You're going to need all your energy for the thrills and spills waiting for you in the next chapter. You're about to follow the course of a raging river all the way from its start until it reaches the sea. Are you ready to go with the flow? Time to put on your life jacket – just in case your canoe capsizes and you end up falling in!

Rivers are a bit like people. They change as they get older. When they're young and just starting out in life, they rush about energetically and are full of get up and, er, flow. As they get older and more mature, they slow down and take things easier, meandering gently through middle age. Finally, old age catches up with them. As they near the sea and their journey's end, many get slow and sleepy, and a bit grumpy if you wake them up suddenly. Sound like anyone you know?

## The river: a turbulent life story

Travis here, welcoming you on my rip-roaring river tour. The trip of a lifetime! A chance to find out what really gets a river flowing. Mind your step as you jump on board!

**Stage 1: Young river.** At this youthful stage, the raging river's really flowing fast. It's a river in a hurry. And it's bursting with youth and energy. It's so strong it can carry horribly heavy rocks which scrape out the shape of its bed and banks.

**Stage 2: Middle age.** The river's starting to slow down now. It can't see the point of all that rushing about. It's dropped the rocks – they're much too heavy – but it still lugs along loads of mud and sand. And instead of smashing straight through obstacles, it sensibly meanders around them. Very grown up.

**Stage 3: Old age.** Now the river's so sluggish and slow it starts to drop off . . . zzzzzz, sorry, it starts to drop off all the mud and sand. Now and again it overflows its banks and floods but then it has to have a good, long rest until finally it flows into the sea.

Stage 1: Young river

Source: OK, folks, good morning and welcome on board. My name's Travis and I'm your tour guide for today. And I don't mind telling you, you're in for a real treat. If you've got any questions, be sure to ask. As long as they're not too difficult!

So here we are at the source of the river - the place where our raging river begins and the start of our turbulent tour. The source might start off as rain falling on a mountain top or springing up from underground. (Water springs up out of the ground like this when the ground isn't "spongy" enough to absorb it.) Is everybody ready and comfy? It's all downhill from now on!

Drainage basin: Hello again. Wakey, wakey! If you look to your left and right, you'll see the river's drainage basin. Sorry, what was that question? Yes, the lad at the back. Oh, I see. No, it's not the thing your mum uses to drain veg or pasta for your tea! It's the land which supplies a river with water. Some rivers have horribly huge drainage basins. The Amazon's covers about 6.5 million square kilometres. That's twice as big as the whole of India. Gi-normous, I think you'll agree!

Tributary: See that little stream flowing in from the right? No, the right, sir, that's the left. Does anyone know what it's called? No? Oh well, never mind.

Geographers call it a tributary. No, madam, I don't know why they can't just say stream either. Believe me, it would make my life easier. But some tributaries are raging rivers in their own right. Take the Amazon again. It's got more than a thousand tributaries. One, the Parana, is among the longest rivers in the world.

Waterfall: And now for the most exciting part of our tour. I love this bit! Is everyone feeling brave? Plucky enough to take the plunge? I'm sorry, madam, it's much too late to turn back now. Even if you're feeling seasick. . . Hold on tight. You're about to have a jaw-dropping ride over a waterfall. A waterfall's where the river plummets over a step of hard rock (see page 64). Close your eyes if you're scared of heights. Here we gooooooooo. . .

39

Stage 2: Middle age

Trunk: Wow! What a splash! We'll just stop here for a minute while I count up and make sure you're all here. Never mind, madam, it can happen to anyone. Now we're on the main bit of the river. Which has nothing to do with elephant's noses or trees. Though you could say that tributaries look a bit like branches growing from a tree trunk. If you were trying to be clever. Or poetic. The trunk is the bit that gives the river its name, like Nile, or Amazon, or, er, D. Get the idea? What's that, sir, you don't understand? I'll be along in a minute to explain.

Valley: See those high-rise slopes on either side? That means we're in a V-shaped river valley. It's been carved out of the rocks by the forceful flow of all that water (see page 57).

You get a splendid view from the top. But you'll need to take another tour for that, we've still got a long way to go. Don't worry, madam, we'll sort you a ticket out later. Put your purse away before it gets wet.

UP STREAM

DOWN STREAM

Meander: Now I know that it seems we're going around in semicircles but rest assured, it's the river, not you, that's going round the bend! These great snaky S-shaped loops you can see in the river are called meanders.

Yes, sir? Good question – why are they called meanders? They're named after the meandering River Menderes in Turkey. No madam, we don't go there on this tour. To meander off course just for a moment, here's a quick diagram to explain how they work:

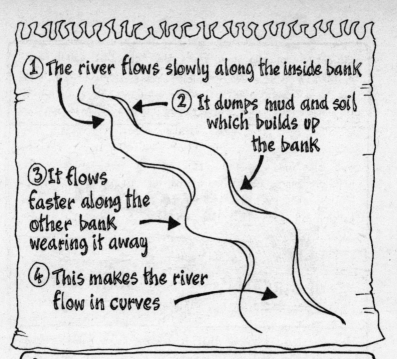

① The river flows slowly along the inside bank

② It dumps mud and soil which builds up the bank

③ It flows faster along the other bank wearing it away

④ This makes the river flow in curves

Ox-bow lake: Look at that lovely banana-shaped lake away to your left? No, not a banana-shaped cake, miss. We'll be having lunch in a very short time. That's right, madam, over there. It's called an ox-bow lake and it's where the river's cut straight across a loopy meander. Anyone want to take a photo? I would if I were you. It'll be no good leaving it till later - the lake may well have dried up by then.

Stage 3: Old age

Floodplain: See all that thick, gooey mud on your left and right? That's the river's floodplain. The mud means that the river's gone and flooded and tipped tonnes of goo all over the land (though other floodplains are covered in sand). It might not look very much, madam, but the mud's packed full of minerals which make brilliant plant food. Fruit and veg just love it. Which is why floodplains make fantastically fertile farms. And talking of food, it's time to stop for lunch!

Mouth: And here we are, folks! The mouth of the river and journey's end! Sadly, this is where we leave our river behind and watch it flow out into the sea. Here it drops the rest of its load of mud and sand. Some of this builds up into a delta (see page 71). Some of it's washed out to sea. And that's where you get off, folks! It's been great meeting you all, and I hope you've enjoyed the trip. Please be careful when leaving the boat. It might take a few moments to get your land legs back. And if you'd like to leave a small-ish tip, I've left a hat at the back. Thank you and see you soon!

## Earth-shattering fact

*Meanders may look bone idle, meandering along without a care in the world. But mind out if a meander's on the move near you. For years, the town of New Harmony in Indiana, USA, stood firmly on the banks of the Wabash River. The river meandered away meekly to the west. True, one loop was heading towards the town but at a snail's pace. There was nothing to worry about. Surely? Then one day in 1984 it started to flow faster, FOUR TIMES FASTER. At this rate, the town would soon be sunk as the river ate away at its foundations. Plans have been made to reroute the river and cut the earth-moving meander off. Will it work? The people of New Harmony are still waiting to see.*

WHERE'S MY RUBBER RING?

## Teacher teaser

Next time a teacher asks you what you want to be when you grow up (boring!), pretend to think hard for a moment, then say:

OH, I'M PLANNING TO BECOME A FAMOUS LIMNOLOGIST

Is that some sort of doctor who treats arms and legs?

## The source of the problem

If your river tour hasn't left you soaked to the skin, think back to the place where it all started. Its source. There are three different types of sauce, sorry, source. No, not tomato sauce, cheese sauce and parsley sauce, or anything else you find lumps of in your school dinner. The *source* of a river is usually high up in mountains.

Can you match these three famous rivers to their sources? Go on – it could be the start of something really big.

Raging rivers to choose from:
**1** River Ganges
**2** River Amazon
**3** River Rhine
Suitable sources to choose from:
**a)** a leaky lake
**b)** a glassy glacier
**c)** a springing mountain stream

**Answers:**

1 b) The source of the Ganges is a glacier in the Himalayas. They're very high mountains in Asia. In spring and summer, the tip of the glacier melts and starts off a stream which grows into the River Ganges. The Ganges flows right across India to the Bay of Bengal in the east. For many people, it's a holy river which fell from heaven and they worship it as a goddess. Below the glacier is a village called Gangotri. Thousands of pilgrims brave the wintery weather to travel here each year to worship the goddess and bathe in the icy river water. Brrr!

2 a) The awesome Amazon starts off as a trickle from a tiny lake high in the Andes mountains in Peru. The trickle flows into a stream called the Apurimac. That's the local word for "great speaker" because of the noise it makes as it roars downhill. From the lake, the Amazon flows right across South America (a staggering distance of 6,440 kilometres) to the Atlantic Ocean. Here it pours so much water into the sea that the sea doesn't start to get salty for another 300 kilometres.

3 a) and c) The raging Rhine begins life as two mountain streams flowing from the Swiss Alps. One glugs from the end of an icy glacier. The other leaks from a lake. The two join forces but they're not alone for long. Lots of other streams muscle in on their act. Then the river flows across Germany and Holland into the North Sea.

## The sorry saga of the search for the Nile's source

You might think that finding the source of a river would be quite simple and straightforward. Surely even a horrible geographer couldn't miss a mountain stream? Especially if the river in question is incredibly long and famous, like the raging River Nile. Easy peasy, you might say. No problem. But you'd be wrong. Horribly wrong.

For hundreds of years, horrible geographers searched high and low for the source of the Nile. They knew that it must be somewhere in Africa, but Africa was a horribly huge country and most of it hadn't yet been explored. Several intrepid expeditions had set off to search for the source (including one sent by the nutty Roman emperor Nero). All of them returned in failure. Where on Earth did the Nile begin? It remained one of geography's best-kept secrets. Until one day in 1856, when two daring British explorers set off for Africa to really get to the source of the problem, once and for all. Their names were Richard Francis Burton (1821–1890) and John Hanning Speke (1827–1864).

GOOD MORNING, SPEKE

ARE YOU SPEAKING TO ME?

## Part I: The search begins
On 19 December 1856, Burton and Speke landed on the island of Zanzibar in the Indian Ocean. From here, they planned to head into Africa where the search would begin. They planned to venture into parts of Africa where no Europeans had ever set foot before.

But they didn't have time to worry. Stocking up for the journey took most of their time. They needed enough supplies to last the whole trip – they reckoned on it taking at least a year – and some porters to carry everything. (They were going to be much too busy exploring to carry anything themselves!) Among all the boxes and boxes of scientific instruments, books, tools and medicines, the two men allowed themselves some small luxuries, including a box of cigars, four sturdy umbrellas and a dozen bottles of brandy. For medicinal purposes, of course.

By June 1857, everything was ready and they finally set sail for Africa. Their route took them inland, then west to Lake Tanganyika. Then they would head north to the mountains to search for the secretive source. For eight hard months, they travelled on.

The heat was horrible, the flies were terrible, and the local people weren't always friendly. But Burton and Speke knew they could put up with almost anything if only they could find the source. Anything, that is, except each other.

The problem was that Burton and Speke were about as alike as chalk and cheese. As happy in each other's company as sausages and lumpy custard. You see, Burton was already a famous explorer, with several expeditions to Africa under his belt. He was brave and brilliant at everything, including speaking 29 languages. But he was also bolshy and looked rather odd. This is how an acquaintance described him:

HE HAD A COUNTENANCE THE MOST SINISTER I HAVE EVER SEEN, DARK CRUEL EYES LIKE A WILD BEAST. HE HAD THE BROW OF A GOD AND THE JAW OF THE DEVIL.

Speke, on the other hand, was boringly neat, tidy and respectable, everything beastly Burton was not. He was also horribly stubborn. He might not be as brainy as Burton, but wasn't about to be bossed about. No way. Burton and Speke just about managed to stick together until they reached Lake Tanganyika but by then they were barely on speaking terms. Fortunately for them both, they were too ill to argue. Burton could hardly move his legs and had such murderous mouth ulcers he could not eat. An illness had left Speke almost blind and he'd gone deaf because of a beetle buried in his ear.

HMM! I WONDER WHAT'S IN EAR?

But what about the source of the Nile, you ask? Had they forgotten why they were there? Who better to spill the beans than Burton? Here's how he might have described the rest of the journey in his secret diary (He did keep a real diary of the expedition but it probably didn't go quite like this.)

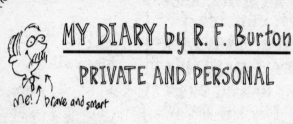

me! / brave and smart

Speke

ugly and dumb!

KEEP OUT! (Especially if your initials are J.H.S.!)

February 1858, Lake Tanganyika, Africa
At last! After eight months of hard slog, we've finally reached Lake Tanganyika. It's really beautiful, I must say. And we're the first Europeans ever to see it. Hooray! Even better, I've been told there's a river flowing from one end of the lake. It's the source of the Nile, you mark my words.

As soon as my mouth ulcers have gone down a bit, I'll be off to have a look. ON MY OWN. Without telling "you-know-who". Hee! Hee!

PS Later... Damn and blast it! You-know-who has had the same idea. That old busy-body's found two canoes and we're about to set off together up the lake. I bet he'll claim he thought of it first.

PPS Still later... We didn't find it. I'm a bit disappointed but I know I'm right. I always am.

September 1858, Kazeh, Africa

You'll never guess what's happened now! That dreadful sneak Speke's been at it again. Trying to make out he's so clever. He's really beginning to annoy me. He only claims that he's found the real source of the Nile... ALL BY HIMSELF! According to him, he's found another lake that he's named after Queen Victoria (What a creep! What does he want, a medal?) and he says that it's definitely the source of the Nile. Of course, it isn't. What a fool! I told you he was being ridiculous. He's just jealous that I beat him to it. When I asked him to prove it was really the source, he got rather twitchy so it's obviously all just a guess. Anyway, I'm sick of it. No one's to mention the "N" word again. As far as I'm concerned, the subject is CLOSED.

May 1859, London, England

This time he's really gone too far. He really has. When we went our separate ways, he PROMISED to wait until I got home to tell people about his stupid theory. I might have known he couldn't keep his word. Grrrr! He's not only gone and told everyone, but they've sent him on another expedition to see if he is right! Well, he's really pulled the wool over their eyes. It makes me so MAD! Don't worry, let him think he's won for now. But I'll be back, and when I am ... I'LL SHOW HIM!!!

September 1864, Bath, England

Speke's gone and done it again! It really is unbelievable! Five years I've waited to get my own back. Five long years. And, guess what, he's only gone and got himself killed! Some people are so selfish. And it wasn't even in Africa. He'd come home, spouting some drivel about the question of the Nile's source being settled, and getting on everyone's nerves. He still hadn't got any proof, you see. (What did I tell you?) So it was decided that he and I would have the whole thing out face to face, man to man, once and for all. We'd fixed the meeting for 16 September when news came that he'd been shot in a hunting accident. The idiot! The lengths some people will go to! (Actually, I'm secretly quite upset but don't ever tell anyone I said so.)

## Part II: The search continues

DAVID LIVINGSTONE...

A JOLLY NICE CHAP

It now fell to Britain's most famous living explorer to take up the search for the source. David Livingstone (1813-1873). Even his name filled people with confidence. Livingstone was ideal for the job. For a start he was terribly nice and got on well with everyone. (Eat your heart out, Burton.)

So, in August 1856, he set sail from England for Africa. Livingstone thought that both Burton and Speke were barking up the wrong tree. He thought that the true source of the Nile was a river to the south. But the expedition to find it was a disaster. Before very long, half of his companions had died, deserted or fallen ill. Livingstone himself was very ill and lost touch with the outside world.

WHEN'S THE NEXT BUS HOME?

HE'S BARKING MAD!

Years went by. Back in Britain, poor old Livingstone had now become Britain's most famous given-up-for-dead explorer. Luckily, people in America hadn't quite given up on him and a journalist from the *New York Herald* newspaper was sent to Africa to find him. (Oh, and to settle the question of the source of the Nile – but you've heard all that before.) His name was Henry Morton Stanley (1841-1904).

To cut a long story short, on 10 November 1871, Stanley finally found Livingstone.

After meeting Livingstone, Stanley was well and truly bitten by the exploration bug. After a short trip to England for fresh supplies, he returned to Africa to check out the claims made by Burton, Speke and Livingstone. And three years later, after many trials, tribulations and horrible hardships, he finally did everyone a favour and solved the mystery of the source of the Nile, once and for all (this time he really did).

So, where on Earth was it? Which one of our three intrepid explorers had been right all along? Was it:

a) Bad-tempered Burton and Lake Tanganyika?
b) Sneaky Speke and Lake Victoria?
c) Long-lost Livingstone and the River Lualba?

**Answer: b)** Speke turned out to have been right all along. (Burton was furious!) The source of the Nile was a river which flowed from Lake Victoria over a waterfall called Ripon Falls. It was bad luck for Burton – he believed that the river flowed from Lake Tanganyika instead. But the river in question flows into the lake, not out of it. And Livingstone might have been good with people but he got his rivers wrong. His River Lualba flows to the south of Lake Victoria. But Stanley later proved that it flows into the colossal River Congo and nowhere near the Nile.

# Raging river fact file

NAME: River Nile
LOCATION: North Africa
LENGTH: 6,695 km
SOURCE: Lake Victoria
DRAINS: 3,349,000 sq km
MOUTH: Flows into the Mediterranean Sea on the coast of Egypt.
FLOW FACTS:

- The longest river on Earth.
- Its two main branches are called the White and Blue Nile because of the colour of their water.
- The Ancient Egyptians lived along its banks.
- What they said about it: "He who once drinks the water of the Nile will return to drink again." (Ancient Egyptian proverb)

55

So, the source of the Nile was found at last. And the riddle of the river was solved. But the story of rivers doesn't stop there. Oh no. The source is only the beginning. Your raging river adventure's got a long way to run. So, dash downstream and into the next chapter. . . .

You may think that rivers aren't good for much except meandering along to the sea. But you're way off course. Even the laziest rivers are hard workers. Running water is horribly powerful. So powerful that, over millions of years, it can change the face of the landscape for ever. (Your teacher's stoniest stare may wipe the smile off your face but even it can't rattle solid rock.) But water doesn't work alone. The river drags along tonnes of rocks, mud and sand which give it its cutting edge. But how on Earth do they do it? Here's a step-by-step guide to earth-moving erosion*.

*That's the tricky technical term for the way rivers run over the ground and gradually grind it down. It can all get horribly wearing!

## How on Earth does erosion work?

1 Horrible geographers always want their own way, like having their own word for everything. But they can't simply call a river a river. That would be far too easy. Take all the rocks and mud a river carries. They can't just call it rocks and mud, they have to call it a load. Boring, or what? The load can be anything from boulders the size of double-decker buses to miniscule grains of sand.

2 Some of the load dissolves in the water. These are the bits that make water hard and leave scaley bits in your kettle. Some bits float along with the water. The biggest rocks and

pebbles sink to the riverbed and roll or bounce along the bottom. Boring geographers call these the bedload.

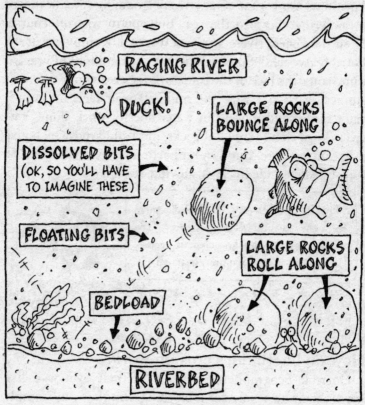

3 Pure water is almost clear and colourless. But who wants a boring river like that? Most rivers are muddy brown. But not all of them. The Yellow River in China is, you've guessed it, yellow! (It's also called the Huang He.) That's because of the tonnes of yellow soil which blow off the land and into the water. Making it so horribly muddy that the Chinese say that if you fall in, you'll never get clean again. (Why not try this next time you need an excuse for not washing?) They also

say, "When the river runs clear," for something that's never likely to happen.

**4** Some of the load scrapes and rubs away at the river's bed and sides, like a giant piece of sandpaper or a scouring pad. (That's a spongy thing for doing the washing up. Ever heard of it?) Other bits bash the rocks up like a huge hammer. No wonder the rocks crumble under the pressure.

**5** The faster a river flows, the bigger and heavier the rocks it can carry and the quicker it grinds the ground down. As the river slows down in middle age, its load grows but is mostly made up of light mud and sand. Near the sea, the river runs out of energy and dumps its load. It can't erode any more land away. It's too much like hard work.

**6** Erosion's often so slow you can't see it happening. To notice the difference, you'd need to stick around for millions of years. This is how long it takes to carve out ghastly gashes in the ground called valleys. They're shaped like the letter "V". (You sometimes get valleys with no river because the river's dried up and left the valley behind.) Gorges are valleys with very steep, sheer sides. Not the places to visit if you suffer from vertigo. (That means you daren't look down.) But if you've got a good head for heights, why not check out our brilliant competition? (Don't set your heart on winning, though.)

THE GREAT

★ GRAND ★

CANYON

COMPETITION

Your chance to win the trip of a lifetime to gawp at the Grand Canyon in Arizona, USA where you can really soak up the atmosphere! A holiday you won't forget in a hurry...

AND GUESS WHO'LL BE YOUR GORGE-OUS TOUR GUIDE?

Prize includes:
* Return tickets for two to Arizona
* A signed copy of Travis's *My Grand Canyon Guidebook*, packed with hints and tips about what to see and do
* A free photo of you with your favourite mule

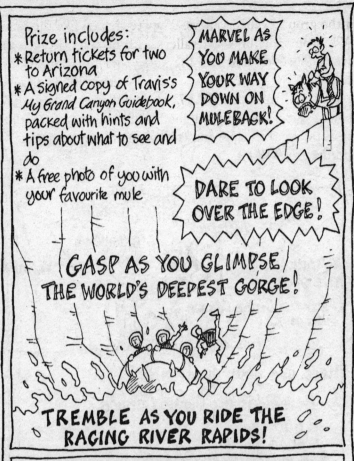

MARVEL AS YOU MAKE YOUR WAY DOWN ON MULEBACK!

DARE TO LOOK OVER THE EDGE!

GASP AS YOU GLIMPSE THE WORLD'S DEEPEST GORGE!

TREMBLE AS YOU RIDE THE RACING RIVER RAPIDS!

TO ENTER, ALL YOU NEED TO DO IS ANSWER THE THREE QUESTIONS OVER THE PAGE – IF YOU DON'T KNOW THE ANSWERS, JUST GUESS. THEN MARK THE GRAND CANYON ON THE MAP. HERE'S A CLUE – YOU'VE ALREADY READ THE ANSWERS!

*HORRIBLE HOLIDAYS – THEY'RE ALL THE RAGE!*

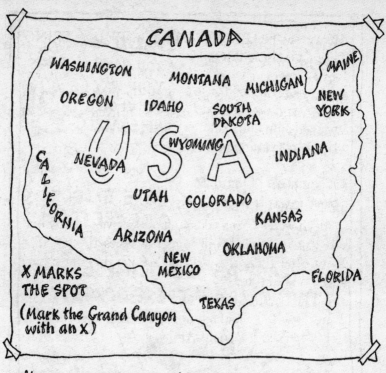

CANADA

WASHINGTON MONTANA MICHIGAN MAINE

OREGON IDAHO SOUTH DAKOTA NEW YORK

U S A WYOMING

NEVADA INDIANA

CALIFORNIA UTAH COLORADO KANSAS

ARIZONA OKLAHOMA

X MARKS THE SPOT

(Mark the Grand Canyon with an X)

NEW MEXICO

TEXAS FLORIDA

Here are your questions:

① How old is the Grand Canyon?
  a: 600 years
  b: 6000 years
  c: 6 million years

② Which river carved out the Grand Canyon?
  a: River Amazon
  b: Colorado River
  c: River Thames

③ How deep is the Grand Canyon?
  a: 1·6 kilometres
  b: 16 kilometres
  c: 160 kilometres

**Answers:** – NO PEEKING IF YOU'RE ENTERING THE COMPETITION!

**1 c)** But the rocks on either side of the Canyon are much, much older than that. Near the top they contain fossils of plants and animals which lived about 250 million years ago. Near the bottom, the rocks date back about 2,000 million years. Ancient or what!

**2 b)** The Colorado River rages along for over 2,000 kilometres from the Rocky Mountains in the USA. It used to flow into the Gulf of California in Mexico but so much water's been taken out of the river for farming and drinking that it no longer reaches the sea. For about 446 kilometres, it flows through the lowest part of the Grand Canyon.

**3 a)** The Grand Canyon is an awesome 1.6 kilometres deep. That's like looking down from the top of a 444-storey building! Ooooh! And it's a pretty sheer drop from the top to the bottom. If you dare make the descent, you can ride down on muleback or hike down on foot. Either way the trip takes several days and you'll need to watch your step – you wouldn't want to disturb a deadly rattlesnake. If you're too tired to climb back up again, why not take a boat downriver. Mind the Big Drops, though: they're the rapids ahead.

Rapids are a stretch of very fast-flowing water. You'll find out how to ride them, and how to survive them, when we get to page 108. You're safe for now!

D'YOU EVER GET THAT SINKING FEELING, SIR?

## Going over the top

But it's not just valleys that feel the full force of raging rivers. Imagine you're a young river. (Go on – you can do it!) You're racing along in full flow when a band of hard rock blocks your way. What do you do? You could either a) keep right on flowing or b) give up and go home? You'll keep going? Good, giving up and going home's for wimps. But get ready for a bumpy ride. If there's softer rock lurking below, you could be about to take the plunge. Here's the inside story of how a waterfall's formed:

1 The river flows over hard rock, with soft rock underneath.
2 Over thousands of years, the water wears the soft rock away.
3 This leaves a little step of hard rock. Which gets bigger . . . and bigger until. . .
4 . . .the raging river plunges over the edge. Splash!

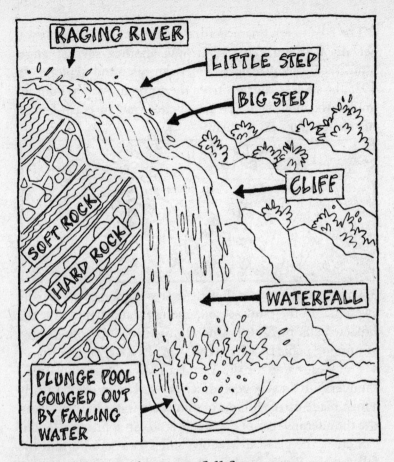

**RAGING RIVER**

**LITTLE STEP**

**BIG STEP**

**CLIFF**

**SOFT ROCK**

**HARD ROCK**

**WATERFALL**

**PLUNGE POOL GOUGED OUT BY FALLING WATER**

**Ten mouth-watering waterfall facts**

1 Think of a building ten storeys high. Then times it by 27. That's how high Angel Falls are and that's a world waterfall record. Angel Falls are the world's highest waterfall. Here, the River Churun plunges 979 metres down the side of Devil's Mountain in Venezuela. *Splashhhhhh!* Big waterfalls often don't wait for land to be slowly eroded so that they can trickle on downwards. They simply plunge off the edge into a valley or gorge below.

**2** The falls weren't named after the rosy-cheeked angels you see on Christmas cards. It was another sort of angel altogether. Jimmy Angel, American pilot and explorer. In 1935, he spotted the falls from the air on his way to hunt for gold in the mountains. To get a better view, he crash-landed his plane right next to them!

**3** The amount of water flowing over some waterfalls is truly awesome. In the rainy season, enough water pours over the Iguacu Falls in South America to fill six Olympic-sized swimming pools EVERY SINGLE SECOND!

**4** The local name for the Victoria Falls is "the smoke that thunders". It's a very good description. The smoke's actually a mist made up of trillions of miniscule water droplets. And the thunderous roar of the water is so ear-splittingly loud it can crack the glass in windows miles away. You'll find the falls on the River Zambezi in Africa but don't forget your earplugs. Pardon?

**5** Compared to Angel Falls, which are 20 times higher, Niagara Falls in North America is small fry. But size isn't everything. This is the most famous waterfall in the world. Everyone wants to take its picture. It's actually two falls on the Niagara River – the Horseshoe Falls on the Canadian side and the American Falls in the USA. They're separated by Goat Island.

**6** Little by little, the world's waterfalls are wearing themselves out as they erode the rocks they splash over. And popular Niagara's no exception. Over the past 12,000 years, it's already gone backwards by 11 whole kilometres. Don't panic, there's still time to visit the Falls. At this rate, horrible geographers reckon, it will take the river another 25,000 years to get back to its source in Lake Erie. Then the Falls will be finished. Shame.

**7** It won't be the first time the Falls have failed. In 1969, the American Falls dried up completely. But this time it was done deliberately. Experts were worried that the Falls were crumbling and they needed to get in and plug the gaps in the rock. They're back to full flow now (the Falls, you fool, not the experts).

**8** Niagara gets millions of visitors. You can gawp at the Falls from Goat Island, brave them from below by boat or take the elevator to the Cave of Winds hidden behind all the falling water. Prepare to get soaked to the skin.

**9** If you're feeling really brave, how about going right over the top and riding over the Falls in a barrel? That's what American teacher, Anna Edson Taylor did. On 24 October 1901, she strapped herself into a large wooden barrel and plunged over the edge. Talk about making a splash! Amazingly, apart from a few cuts and bruises, she wasn't seriously hurt. If you were thinking of getting your own teacher to give it a go, bad luck. All dangerous stunts were banned in 1911.

**10** Intrepid Miss Taylor was just one of many brave (or barking mad) souls who tried to cross the Falls in weird and wonderful ways.

The barmiest was fearless Frenchman, Jean-François Gravelet (1824–1897), better known as the great Blondin (it means "Blondie"). Want to read all about his daredevil adventures? We've looked in our records and dug out an old copy of *The Daily Globe* to fill you in on the story.

# The Daily Globe

## 20 August 1859, Niagara Falls

# HIGH-WIRE HIGH JINKS AT NIAGARA

Cheering crowds lined Niagara Falls yesterday to witness a truly death-defying feat. In front of thousands of nervous on-lookers, the world famous acrobat, Blondin, walked across the Falls on a tightrope . . . carrying his manager, Mr Harry Colcord, on his back! Even though Mr Colcord was almost twice his weight!

ROOM FOR ONE MORE ON TOP

Mr Colcord was later heard to say, "Never again! It was a nightmare from beginning to end. That bloomin' Blondin nearly lost his balance at least six times! From now on, I'm keeping my feet firmly on the ground!" He wasn't the only one to have suffered a fright. Several spectators were so shocked they fainted.

This is not the first time that brave Blondin has performed his daring stunt. He made his first tightrope crossing early this year on a rope stretched 50 metres above the raging waters. On that occasion, his hair-raising hike took just under 20 minutes including a stop for a glass or two of wine. He enjoyed it so much, he came back for more.

Blondin crossed the Falls several more times, once blindfolded and once pushing a passenger along in a wheelbarrow.

ALONG FOR THE RIDE

When asked if he was ever scared, he replied, "Non (no). My father taught me how to walk ze tightrope when I was five years old. I've been doing crazy zings ever since. It is no more to me than a stroll down the Champs-Elysées."*

After this latest crossing, our on-the-spot reporter managed to snatch a few words with Blondin before he was mobbed by his adoring fans. He asked him if he'd be having another go. "Bien sûr (Of course)," Blondin replied, "I shall be back. And ze next time, I'm hoping to cross ze tightrope on stilts." Well, everyone at *The Daily Globe* wishes him bonne chance (good luck)!

* The Champs-Elysées is a famous street in Paris.

## Treading a very fine line

His high jinx at Niagara earned Blondin fame and fortune, though some people had their doubts. The newpapers of the time (though not our own *Daily Globe*!) called him "a fool who ought to be arrested". But Blondin braved it out. He hadn't done badly for someone who'd started his career as a child star called the Little Wonder. But it didn't stop with stilts. In all, he crossed the Falls 17 times. Without ever falling off! Once, he stopped half way, sat down on the rope, got out a small stove and, cool as a cucumber, cooked himself an omelette! Oh well, you know what they say, food always tastes better outdoors!

## Lightening the load

After all the excitement, it's high time to slow things down a bit and return to our raging river. Except it's not quite the force it used to be. It's slower and hasn't enough energy to lug its load any longer. So it dumps it at its big mouth. If the tides are strong enough, some of the load's washed out to sea. But some of it builds up into new land. The river has to branch out to flow round it, turning the river mouth into a massive maze of streams and islands called a delta. Time to dazzle your teacher with some in-depth delta data. . .

Deltas were given their name by a horrible Ancient Greek historian called Herodotus. He spent a lot of his time travelling around Egypt taking notes for his new book. And one thing he noticed was that the mouth of the River Nile was triangular-shaped, a bit like the Greek letter D, or delta, which the Ancient Greeks wrote like this Δ. And the triangle thing has stuck. But you know horrible geographers. They're always meddling. So now they've come up with three delta shapes:

**1** Bow shaped. The posh Latin name for this is arcuate (ark-you-ate) which means arched or bent like a bow. Officially, this is the shape of the Nile delta. Unofficially, the Ancient Egyptians said their delta was shaped like a lotus blossom. Lovely!

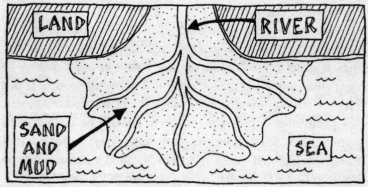

**2** Pointy. The posh Latin name for this is cuspate which means shaped like a point or a peak. Remember Romulus, Remus and the bloody story of Rome? Well, the River Tiber (which Rome stands on) ends up in a pointy delta.

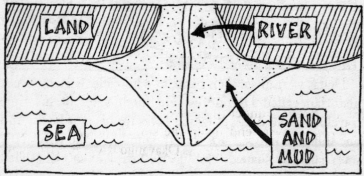

**3 Bird's foot.** Doesn't have a posh Latin name but you can guess its shape. It has lots of branches which look like the toes on a bird's foot. The Mississippi delta is this shape.

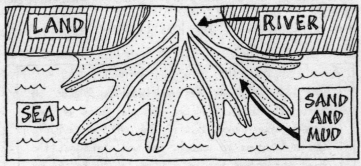

CAN YOU SPOT THE DIFFERENCE?

Some deltas are mind-bogglingly big. The delta of the River Ganges is gigantic, almost as big as England and Wales put together. And talking of BIG, one of the islands in the Amazon delta is about the same size as Switzerland. Some deltas are still growing. Each year, the Mississippi River dumps almost 500 million tonnes of mud and sand at its delta, pushing it further and further out to sea. As you saw on your tour, all this land is fabulously rich and fertile, so it's great for growing fruit and veg. But people living on big deltas run a big risk. Because the land's so flat and low-lying, it quickly goes under if the river floods.

Not all rivers end up in the sea. Some flow into lakes. Even more extraordinary, the Okavango River in Africa sinks into the Kalahari Desert sands. Sounds a bit dry? It's all change in the rainy season when the river floods. Then the desert delta becomes a maze of steamy swamps and sleepy lagoons, lined with tall tangles of reeds. A perfect hiding place for thousands of river-loving animals like fish eagles, hippos and crocodiles.

And me! It's one of my favourite places on Earth, though those hippos can play havoc if they capsize your canoe. But if it's wild river wildlife you're wanting to watch, and you can't get the time off school for an African safari, follow me into the next chapter. But be warned. This is not for the faint-hearted. If the sight of a spider makes you shiver or if you stand on a chair at the merest glimpse of a mouse, you may want to go away and do something else, like your homework, for the next few pages. . .

Rivers are wonderful places for watching wildlife. But are they such great places for wildlife to live? For hundreds of river plants and animals, raging river living isn't all plain sailing. A river is a horribly risky place to live. For a start, it depends which bit of the river you choose to live in. . .

## Beginning

The water's cold and fast-flowing and there's not much to eat. But there's plenty of oxygen to breathe in the bubbling water (provided the current doesn't knock you off your feet).

## Middle

The river's flowing more slowly now so water plants can take root in its sandy bottom. Bugs hide their ugly mugs among the plants, until they're snapped up by hungry fish.

BURP!

## End

The river's slow and sluggish and the water's warmer. In some places, it's almost slowed to a halt. This is great for animals like water beetles that usually live in still-water ponds. They feel right at home.

## Creature features

What do you need to survive a tiring day at school? Several cans of pop? A few bags of crisps? A long snooze through double geography? Just like you, river creatures need certain things to survive. (Come to think of it, you need all of these things too.) They are:

• Oxygen to breathe
• Food to eat
• A way of getting from A to B
• A safe place to shelter (or at least something to hang on to).

So how on Earth do they do it? Many creatures have special features to help them. Some are stranger than others. Some are downright dippy. To find out more, why not try this queasy quiz.

### Dead or Alive?

We've given the creatures on the next page special features to help them survive in the river. If you think they are true, say ALIVE! If you think they are false, say DEAD! Think hard. It could be a matter of life or death.

1 Fish carry oxygen in tanks on their backs. DEAD OR ALIVE?

2 Matamata turtles breathe through snorkels. DEAD OR ALIVE?

3 The archer fish uses a bow and arrow to shoot its food. DEAD OR ALIVE?

4 Caddis fly larvae catch their food in nets. DEAD OR ALIVE?

5 Some fish love eating poo. DEAD OR ALIVE?

6 Some worms spend their whole lives with their heads in the sand. DEAD OR ALIVE?

7 Catfish cling on to rocks with their lips. DEAD OR ALIVE?

8 Dippers are birds that hate the water. DEAD OR ALIVE?

---

**Answers:**

1 DEAD! Fish breathe oxygen dissolved in the water, not tucked away in tanks on their backs. But they don't breathe through lungs like you or me. Instead they have slitty gills on the sides of their heads. You know how fish make funny popping noises with their mouths? (Open and close your mouth quickly and you'll get the idea.) This shows that they're still breathing. As the fish swims along, it closes its gills, opens its mouth and gulps in water. Then it closes its mouth, opens its gills and pushes the water out over them. Oxygen from the water goes into the fish's blood. Simple.

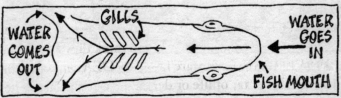

**2 ALIVE!** The matamata turtle lurks on the bottom of muddy rivers but, not being a fish, it needs to breathe oxygen from the air. So it sticks its long neck up out of the water so its nostrils and mouth can reach for air. This way it can also snap up passing fish before they notice it's there! Cunning.

**3 DEAD!** Archer fish don't use bows and arrows but they do have a cunning trick up their fins. They shoot down air-borne insects and insects feeding on vegetation above the water's surface with a well-aimed . . . glob of spit! Don't try this at home, kids!

**4 ALIVE!** Caddis fly larvae, or bugs, live in fast-flowing rivers where there isn't much food to go round. But this isn't a problem for these ugly bugs. They spin weeny webs between two pebbles and wait for tiny, tasty creatures to be swept downstream for dinner.

**5 ALIVE!** I'm sorry to say it's true. In fact, many revolting river creatures eat other creatures' poo. It all starts when dead leaves fall in the river from overhanging trees. They're crunched up by creatures like caddis fly larvae and crayfish. And it's their faeces (that's the posh word for poo) that our foul fish love to feast on.

6 ALIVE! Tubifex worms spend their whole lives with their heads in the mud on the river bottom. Why? Well, they sift food from the mud with their mouths and wave their tails about to collect oxygen. They just do it upside down. Weird or what!

7 ALIVE! Getting a grip in a fast-flowing river can be difficult at the best of times. Many creatures have hooks or suckers for holding on to slippery rocks. But catfish have a crazier way of coping. They give the rock a great big sloppy kiss and hang on with their luscious lips!

8 DEAD! Dippers love water, the faster the better. Otherwise, they'd starve. This dippy bird lives on larvae. To catch its supper, it dives underwater then walks along the river bottom flicking its wings to keep its balance and picking its food off the rocks. Its thick, oily feathers keep it warm and waterproof.

That's all very well, I hear you say, but isn't it a teeny bit tame? I mean, spitting fish and bashful worms are fine if you like that sort of thing. But it's kids' stuff. What about something meaner and moodier? OK, if you're sure. . . For the wettest, wildest wildlife in water, head for the awesome River Amazon. But be careful. Some of the creatures you're about to meet can turn nasty. Very nasty. Especially if they haven't had their lunch. Still keen to go? Well, don't say I didn't warn you.

## Raging river fact file

NAME: River Amazon
LOCATION: South America
LENGTH: 6,400 km
SOURCE: Andes Mountains, Peru
DRAINS: 7,050,000 sq km
MOUTH: Flows into the Atlantic Ocean in Brazil
FLOW FACTS:

• It's the biggest river on Earth with the most water.
• It's got at least 1000 known tributaries (and there may be many more waiting to be found out).
• It's home to at least 1,500 types of fish. That's ten times more than in all the rivers in Europe put together! And more than in the entire Atlantic.
• The world's largest rainforest grows along its banks.

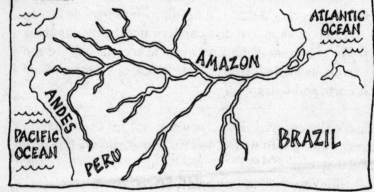

# Some Amazonian animals to avoid

Travis here. I'm glad I caught you before you left. If you're determined to attempt this foolhardy adventure, I won't try to stop you. But at least let me put you in the picture. I've been helping the police with their enquiries about tracking down the most dangerous Amazonian animals. Here are my own secret files on the worst culprits. Read and digest, before they digest you!

## Name: ELECTRIC EEL

**Description:** A knife-shaped fish, 2m long. A very sharp character.

**Known Crimes:** Attacking and killing unsuspecting fish and frogs (and humans).

**Methods Used:** Now this bit's really shocking, the eel zaps its prey with electricity (made in its tail). The shock only lasts a second but it takes the eel an hour to recharge its batteries.

**Known Enemies:** None really. It sees off predators in the same shocking way.

**Eyewitness Account:**

> I do not remember having ever received a more dreadful shock. I was affected during the rest of the day with a violent pain in my knees and almost every joint.

Alexander Von Humboldt, Scientist 1769-1859

81

# Name: ANACONDA

**Description:** The world's biggest snake. This raging reptile grows 10 metres long and measures a metre round its middle. (Imagine giving one a hug!) Even its scales are bigger than thumbnails.

**Known Crimes:** Killing prey as big as deer, goats and caimans (they're close relations to crocodiles). Don't panic-(most) humans aren't tasty enough to be tried.

**Methods Used:** Inflicts a crushing blow with its coils, literally squeezing its victim to death. Then it swallows it whole. Gulp!

**Known Disguises:** Lurks along the riverbank lying in wait for prey. Completely hidden by the water apart from its nostrils and eyes.
Then it pounces.
It's also good at climbing trees and pretending to be a harmless branch.

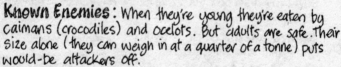

**Known Enemies:** When they're young they're eaten by caimans (crocodiles) and ocelots. But adults are safe. Their size alone (they can weigh in at a quarter of a tonne) puts would-be attackers off.

**Note:** If you're bitten by an anaconda, don't pull your arm out at once. Instead, push it further down into the snake's mouth. The anaconda's teeth slant inwards. When the sneaky snake lets go for a second to get a better grip, pull like mad!

# Name: PIRANHA

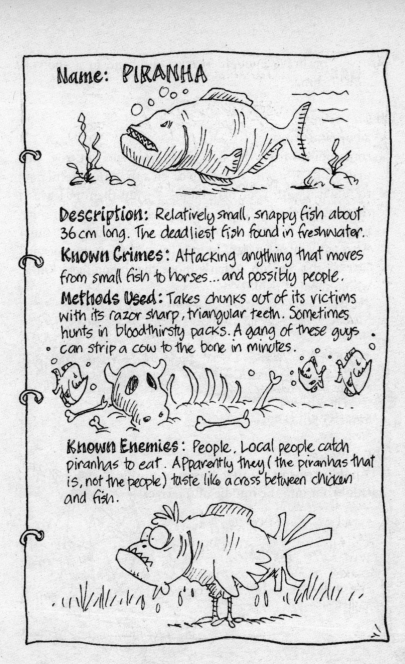

**Description:** Relatively small, snappy fish about 36 cm long. The deadliest fish found in freshwater.

**Known Crimes:** Attacking anything that moves from small fish to horses... and possibly people.

**Methods Used:** Takes chunks out of its victims with its razor sharp, triangular teeth. Sometimes hunts in bloodthirsty packs. A gang of these guys can strip a cow to the bone in minutes.

**Known Enemies:** People. Local people catch piranhas to eat. Apparently they (the piranhas that is, not the people) taste like a cross between chicken and fish.

Are you be brave enough to try your hand at a spot of piranha fishing?

*What you need:*
- a bow and arrow
- some poison from the skin of an arrow-poison frog. To make your own, you'll need to catch a frog. Be careful not to touch it with your bare hands – wrap them in leaves, that's what the locals do. Then stick it on a skewer and roast it over a fire so the poison's squeezed out. Alternatively, ask a local hunter (nicely) for some poison. Just a drop will do – that's more than enough to kill a whole shoal of fish!

- a watertight canoe

*What you do:*
1 Dip the arrow in the frog poison.
2 Paddle out into the middle of the river.

3 Take aim and . . . fire.

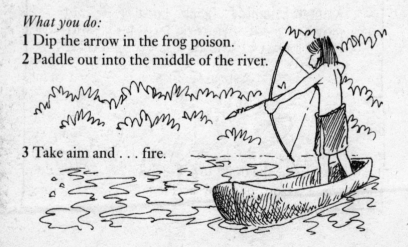

**4** Mind your fingers as you pull the fish in.

Recipe idea: To make freaky fish fingers, dip the piranhas in batter and lightly fry. Don't eat the teeth.

Note: There are some people who say that piranhas have had a very raw deal and don't deserve their ravenous reputation. They claim that they're actually rather friendly fish who prefer a snack of fruit and veg. Pah! I bet they'd be the first to run a mile if a piranha suggested a poolside barbeque!

One man who would probably have given his right arm for a freshly cooked piranha fish finger was one-eyed Spanish soldier and explorer, Francisco de Orellana (about 1490-1546). In fact, anything tasty to eat would have done very nicely. Get your teeth into this terrible tale of how fishy Francisco became the first European to sail all the way down the River Amazon, quite by accident, and largely on an empty stomach!

## Up the Amazon without a paddle, sometime in 1540-1541

The Spanish had arrived in South America in 1540 with one thing on their mind – GOLD! They weren't interested in rivers or wildlife. No. They wanted to get rich quick. And they didn't care how they did it. Their greedy leader was a man called Gonzalo Pizarro who happened to be Francisco's cousin. After weeks of marching, with not a gold nugget in sight, they finally reached the River Napo, exhausted and . . . ravenously hungry. They'd polished off their food rations, followed by their horses, pigs and hunting dogs. Now there was hardly anything left to eat. So Pizarro sent Francisco and 50 soldiers off in search of fresh supplies. "And don't be long," he told them, having to raise his voice over the sound of his rumbling tummy. "I'm starving." Guess what? He never saw them again.

Francisco didn't mean to leave his cousin in the lurch. Well, not at first. He really meant to stock up and sail back. Honest. Or so he said. But after a week in a bumpy old boat, he didn't have the stomach for the return journey. Who says blood is thicker than water? Instead, he and his men carried on rowing and stumbled on an enormous river. It was so huge they thought at first it must be the sea. In fact, they had found the Amazon. By following the river, they reckoned they'd eventually reach the Atlantic Ocean and from there they'd sail for Spain. Home, sweet home.

Getting to the Atlantic wasn't all plain sailing. For a start, they had no idea of the length of the awesome Amazon. It just seemed to go on and on. And the local people weren't always pleased to see them. No wonder – when forceful Francisco wanted supplies, he simply captured a village and helped himself. There was plenty of time to think of a name for the river. But what to choose? In the end, he called it after a band of wild women warriors he claimed had attacked them with bows and arrows. They reminded him of the fierce female fighters of Greek legend called the Amazons.

AMAZING!

NO, AMAZONS

(Oddly enough, no one else ever saw them so no one could say if he was right or wrong.) Anyway, to cut a long river short, 4,750 kilometres and eight months later, the Spaniards finally reached the sea.

What became of fearless Francisco when he got home? Was he in deep trouble for doing the dirty on his friends? Not a bit of it. His adventures were thought so exciting that the king let him off the hook. In fact, Francisco was promoted and sent back to the Amazon to claim the land for Spain. But he never made it. After all he'd been through – the heat, the flies, fiery "Amazons" – his ship went and capsized at the mouth of the river, and he drowned.

As for poor old Pizarro (remember him?), well, he waited for weeks for cousin Francisco to return. When it finally dawned on him that they weren't going to show up, he and his men hungrily began to retrace their steps to the city of Quito in Ecuador. By this time, they'd been reduced to a desperate diet of snakes, insects and even their own leather belts and saddles, boiled in water flavoured with herbs. Mmm, chewy. Of the 350 men who first set out, so many had starved to death, dropped through disease or ended up as dinner for alligators and jaguars that only 80 made it back to Quito.

*Earth-shattering fact*
*Everything about the Amazon is larger-than-life. Take water lilies, for instance. Forget the titchy things you see floating in your dad's garden pond. These leaves are LARGE, with a capital L.A.R.G.E. Plenty large enough for your little sister to lounge about on. Don't worry about her falling in – the leaves are full of spaces which fill with air (like leafy balloons) and keep the leaf bobbing upright in the water. (Oh, you weren't worried, sorry!) Sharp thorns underneath stop the leaves being nibbled by passing fish and getting a pesky puncture!*

# Get wet gardening

If you're planning on planting up your own river and don't know which fluvial foliage to choose, look no further. Help is at hand with our very own green-fingered guide to riverside gardening. And if you can't tell your weeds from your water lilies, who better to turn to for advice than Travis's very own Auntie Flo.

PAPYRUS

DESCRIPTION: A TALL GRASS-LIKE PLANT. INCREDIBLY USEFUL. THE ANCIENT EGYPTIANS MADE PAPYRUS PAPER, MATS, SANDALS AND SAILS. IT'S ALSO GOOD FOR FUEL.

POSITION: SWAMPY GROUND ALONG THE RIVERBANK.

A LOVELY LOOKING PLANT THIS, AND IF YOU LEAVE IT ALONE IT'LL GROW VERY FAST, BUT DON'T LET THE SOIL GET TOO DRY. IT'S ALMOST DIED OUT IN EGYPT BECAUSE SO MUCH WATER'S BEEN DRAINED FROM THE NILE.

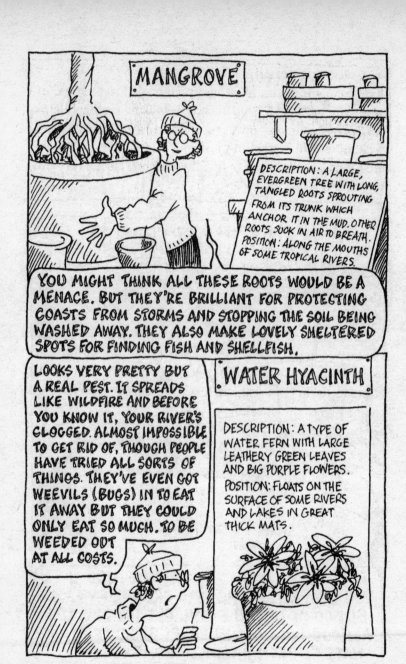

# MANGROVE

DESCRIPTION: A LARGE, EVERGREEN TREE WITH LONG, TANGLED ROOTS SPROUTING FROM ITS TRUNK WHICH ANCHOR IT IN THE MUD. OTHER ROOTS SUCK IN AIR TO BREATH.
POSITION: ALONG THE MOUTHS OF SOME TROPICAL RIVERS.

YOU MIGHT THINK ALL THESE ROOTS WOULD BE A MENACE. BUT THEY'RE BRILLIANT FOR PROTECTING COASTS FROM STORMS AND STOPPING THE SOIL BEING WASHED AWAY. THEY ALSO MAKE LOVELY SHELTERED SPOTS FOR FINDING FISH AND SHELLFISH.

LOOKS VERY PRETTY BUT A REAL PEST. IT SPREADS LIKE WILDFIRE AND BEFORE YOU KNOW IT, YOUR RIVER'S CLOGGED. ALMOST IMPOSSIBLE TO GET RID OF, THOUGH PEOPLE HAVE TRIED ALL SORTS OF THINGS. THEY'VE EVEN GOT WEEVILS (BUGS) IN TO EAT IT AWAY BUT THEY COULD ONLY EAT SO MUCH. TO BE WEEDED OUT AT ALL COSTS.

# WATER HYACINTH

DESCRIPTION: A TYPE OF WATER FERN WITH LARGE LEATHERY GREEN LEAVES AND BIG PURPLE FLOWERS.
POSITION: FLOATS ON THE SURFACE OF SOME RIVERS AND LAKES IN GREAT THICK MATS.

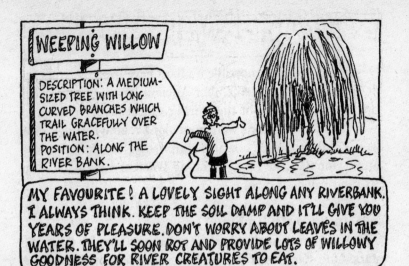

WEEPING WILLOW

DESCRIPTION: A MEDIUM-SIZED TREE WITH LONG CURVED BRANCHES WHICH TRAIL GRACEFULLY OVER THE WATER.
POSITION: ALONG THE RIVER BANK.

MY FAVOURITE! A LOVELY SIGHT ALONG ANY RIVERBANK. I ALWAYS THINK. KEEP THE SOIL DAMP AND IT'LL GIVE YOU YEARS OF PLEASURE. DON'T WORRY ABOUT LEAVES IN THE WATER. THEY'LL SOON ROT AND PROVIDE LOTS OF WILLOWY GOODNESS FOR RIVER CREATURES TO EAT.

But peckish piranhas, shocking eels and whopping great water lilies aren't the only weird wildlife you'll find near rivers. There's something far stranger lurking among the water weeds. What's that? Horrible humans, of course! Read about them in the next chapter.

# RAGING-RIVER LIVING.

Despite the dangers, horrible humans have lived by rivers for thousands of years. Remember Ancient Rome-by-the river? It's not alone. Some of the world's oldest towns, cities and even whole civilizations were built along raging rivers. Rivers were, and still are, horribly important for humans. So important that the time-watching Ancient Egyptians even set their calendar by one. . .

## Setting a date for it

The Egyptians usually worked out their calendar from the stars. One star, in particular. The year began in June when Sirius, the dog star, appeared in the sky. OK, you say, so maybe they were top astronomers but what on Earth has all this got to do with rivers? Well, Sirius also marked the start of the River Nile's yearly flood. This happened when heavy spring rain and melting snow upriver in the mountains of Ethiopia poured massive amounts of water into the Nile. By June, the flow had reached Egypt. When the water went down, it left lots of lovely, thick, crumbly black soil behind which the green-fingered Egyptians grew bumper crops in.

But the river was more than a handy way of remembering to invite your friends round for a New Year's Eve party. It was vital to life in Ancient Egypt. You see Ancient Egypt was mostly dry, dusty desert where, green fingers or not, nothing would grow. Without the reviving River Nile, there would have been no food to eat, no water to drink, no way of travelling to visit your relatives, no relatives to visit, and no horrible Ancient Egyptian history to learn. . .

To see just how much the Egyptians relied on their remarkable river, try turning back the clocks. Imagine you're an Egyptian farmer. Why not call yourself Hapi (for boys) or Anukis (for girls) to help you feel the part?

Good choices if I may say so. Hapi was the god of flooding. Anukis was the goddess of the First Cataract (a series of rapids) on the Nile.

Here's what a year in your life might have been like:

# 1 June–October: the river floods

The raging river's in full flood now and your fields are under water. You hire the fields from a wealthy landlord who takes a cut of your crops. Luckily for you, they're right by the edge of the river, the best place for them to be. Too far back and the flood might not reach them. But the flood puts a stop to farming. Time to put your feet up for a bit? No way. During the flood, the government sends ordinary farmers like you off to help build pyramids and tombs for the king.

I WISH I WAS BACK ON THE FARM!

# 2 October–March: get those seeds sown

You're back from the building site and the floods are falling. Before you know it, it's all go down on the farm. You plough your fields with your wooden plough, pulled by two faithful oxen. If you're very poor, you'll have to pull the plough yourself. Then you sow handfuls of seed in the rich river soil and get ready for a non-stop round of weeding and watering. It's back-breaking work.

I WISH HE WAS BACK ON THE BUILDING SITE!

## 3 March–June: bring in the harvest before going back to 1

Time to sharpen your sickle (a long knife made from flintstone) and set about harvesting your crops. The taxman will be here soon to work out how much you can keep for yourself and pay to your landlord, and how much you owe to the king. If you can't pay up, you'll be beaten. And before you snatch a well-earned rest, don't forget to patch up the canals which carry water from the river into your fields. Otherwise, you'll be left high and dry.

**Teacher teaser**

Send your teacher into a rage with this excuse for missing double geography:

What on Earth are you going to do?

The Nile doesn't flood anymore because of the awesome Aswan Dam which now keeps the flow in check. The good news is that Egypt no longer gets devastatingly destructive floods. The bad news is that no more floods means no more free rich black soil.

So farmers have to fork out for chemical fertilizers to refresh their tired fields. Not only are these costly, they can poison the river water. It's a watered–down blessing.

### River living – the watery truth

Despite the changes, some 50 million people still rely on the Nile for keeping them alive. And they're not the only ones. Millions of people all over the world depend on life-saving rivers. So why on Earth do they do it? Why is river living all the rage? What do rivers have to offer that you don't get from dry land? Some people rave on about the views. Others rant about finding rivers relaxing. But the real reason why humans live near raging rivers is . . . raging river water.

*All living things are made up mostly of water. Including horrible humans. Are you as wet as a lettuce? Not quite. A lettuce leaf is 95 per cent water. A potato's 80 per cent. You come in third at 70 per cent, but that still means that you're two thirds water. Which two thirds could that be?*

## Wonderful water

How much water do you use in a day? You've probably never given it a second thought. Well, prepare to be amazed. The answer is a lavish 150 litres. That's about the same as two big bathtubsful or 600 cans of pop!

I THOUGHT I'D SAVE WATER

Here are just some of the things you can do with all this horrible $H_2O$. You can:

• **Drink it**. Water is absolutely vital for life. Without it, you'd literally die of thirst in a few days. But did you know that most drinking water comes from raging rivers? If you want a thirst-quenching glass of water, you simply turn on the tap. But how on Earth did the water get there in the first place? Here's how you get water on tap:

1 A dam is built across a river. . .

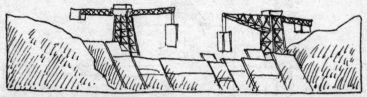

2 . . .forming a big lake called a reservoir.

3 The water's piped from here to the waterworks where it's cleaned and made safe to drink.

4 First, the water flows through a screen to filter out twigs, leaves and branches.

5 Then it soaks through a bed of fine sand to filter out any dirt.

6 A gas called chlorine's added to kill any germs.

7 Then the clean water's piped underground and through smaller pipes into your home.

> **Dirty Water Warning**
> *You're one of the lucky ones. In poorer parts of the world, many people's drinking water comes straight from the river. And because the river doubles up as a toilet and a rubbish dump, it's often horribly dirty and jam-packed with ghastly germs. They can spread deadly water-borne diseases like cholera or dysentery, and can cause severe diarrhoea. To make matters worse, people often have to walk miles and miles to collect their dirty water each day. Think about that next time you turn on the tap.*

• **Wash in it.** Keeping clean uses hundreds of litres of river water a day. You use about 80 litres every time you have a bath, 10 litres when you flush the toilet and about 100 litres for every load in the washing machine.

**a)** Have a shower instead of a bath. It'll save about 50 litres of water. (Of course, skipping both saves even more but you might end up ponging a bit.)

**b)** Don't leave the tap running when you clean your teeth. (But don't forget to keep brushing twice a day.)
**c)** Put half a brick in your toilet cistern. (Ask permission first!) It'll cut down the water you use to flush the loo by about a third. (Don't worry, it'll still do the job.)

• **Water your fields with it.** Farming is horribly thirsty work. Growing a 1 kilogram bag of rice uses 35 bathtubs of water! Goodness knows how much bathwater it took to cook your school dinner. Some of the richest farmland in the world lies around river deltas where there's always a good water supply. Take the delta of the River Mekong in Vietnam. It's like a gigantic rice field where half the country's rice is grown. Sometimes the water needs a helping hand. It's pumped and sprinkled on fields, brought by canal or is even controlled by computer. The posh name for this is irrigation.

The Ancient Egyptians knew all about irrigation. They used an ingenious device called a shaduf to freshen up their fields. It was simple but brilliant. In fact, it worked so well that it's still going strong today. Are you nimble-fingered enough to make your own full-sized shaduf?

*What you need:*
- three strong canes about 1.5 metres long
- one strong cane about 1.75 metres long
- some rope or strong string
- one small bucket
- a carrier bag of sand (Note: to decide how big the bag needs to be, fill the bucket with water. The bag needs to weigh the same.)
- a strong adult to help you

*What you do:*
1 Tie the three canes together to make a tepee shape.

2 Stand your tepee firmly in the ground.
3 Tie the middle of the longer cane to the top of the tepee. This cane becomes the lever.
4 Tie your bucket to one end. . .
5 . . .and your bag of sand to the other to weigh it down.

*How it works:*

Farmers use a shaduf to lift water from the river into their fields. First they push the weighted end up to lower the bucket into the water. Then they pushed it down to raise the full bucket. Simple, eh! This means that one farmer can lift thousands of litres of water on his own, in a day. It's much quicker and easier than filling buckets by hand (and saves all that bending over). Don't forget to ask permission before you try out your shaduf on your dad's prize-winning veg!

- **Catch your dinner in it.**

1 Forget high-tech fishing boats, full of mod cons. Forget fishing rods, hooks and lines. Try fishing the River Amazon way. There, fishermen beat the water with bundles of vines until their poisonous juice oozes out. This kills the fish and they float to the surface where they're scooped up in baskets and nets. Cunning!

**2** You'd need a basket the size of a small boat to catch a pirarucu. It's the biggest river fish. It lives in the Amazon and weighs a whopping 200 kilograms. That's over four times heavier than you! People eat it dried or salted. Apparently it tastes a bit like cod.

**3** If you can't get to a river, bring a river into your home. Some farmers in the Mekong River delta keep catfish under the living room floor! Their houses are built on stilts over the river. Every day, they open a trapdoor in the floor and feed the fish to fatten them up for market. (Don't try this at home, kids. Stick to goldfish instead!)

• **Light up your house with it.** Next time you turn on the light, think about where all that electricity comes from. The answer might be, you've guessed it, a river. About a fifth of all our electricity comes from raging rivers. It's cheap, clean and it won't run out. To get at it, you need a raging river and a dam. As the water flows through the dam, it turns the blades of a wheel called a turbine. In turn it drives a shaft which drives a generator to generate electricity.

Got it? Technically it's called hydro-electricity (hydro means water). It's best if the river's raging downhill, so Niagara Falls is really humming.

• **Run your factory with it.** How much water does it take to make a car? Go on, have a guess, it's not a trick question. The answer is about 50 bathtubsful. That's how much water a steelworks uses to make a car's worth of steel. Factories need huge amounts of water to turn raw materials into the goods we use. It's used for processing the materials. This means cleaning them, mixing them and cooling them down. That's why many factories are built near rivers so they can use the water. Take the raging River Rhine for example. . .

## Raging river fact file

NAME: River Rhine

LOCATION: Central Europe

LENGTH: 1,390 km

SOURCE: Two small streams in the Swiss Alps

DRAINS: 220,000 sq km

MOUTH: Flows into the North Sea near Rotterdam in Holland

FLOW FACTS:

● Because it runs right across the heart of Europe, through many leading industrial countries, it's the busiest river in the world. There's a constant stream of tugs and barges carrying steel, iron ore, coal, timber, petrol and other heavy cargoes.

● Rotterdam is the world's busiest seaport. Each year, it handles about 300 million tonnes of cargo and about 30,000 ships dock there.

● The River Ruhr is a tributary of the Rhine. Its banks are lined with hundreds of factories making chemicals, iron, steel, cars and computers.

> **Dirty Water Warning**
> By 1970, factories and farms had poured so much filth into the Rhine that the rancid river was declared DEAD! A massive clean-up began. Then, in 1986, things went from bad to worse. Fire broke out at a chemical factory in Switzerland, leaking 30 toxic tonnes of poison straight into the river. This lethal cocktail turned the river bright red and killed half a million fish. Horrible. Parts of the river were closed off and the clean-up campaign had to start all over again.

## Messing about on the river

Anything else you can do with a raging river? Mess about on it, of course. (Be careful, though, rivers can be dangerous places.) If you're longing for a spot of fast-flowing fun, why not pay a visit to the village of Flowing-oh-so-slowly which is holding its annual sports day?

VILLAGE NEWS BOARD

The village of Flowing oh-so-slowly is proud to present its...

☆ ANNUAL RAGING RIVER SPORTS DAY ☆

Come along and make a Splash!

EVERYBODY WELCOME (what ever your watersport)

ALL WINNERS GUARANTEED A FABULOUS PRIZE

TURN THE PAGE AND CHOOSE A SPORT →

ANGLING

SEE IF YOU CAN BEAT THE WORLD RECORD FOR THE MOST FISH CAUGHT - 625 IN A DAY!

ROWING

MIND YOU DON'T CATCH A CRAB! THAT'S THE TECHNICAL TERM FOR GETTING YOUR OAR STUCK IN THE WATER

SWIMMING

DON'T GET CARRIED AWAY BY THE CURRENT!

CANOEING

DON'T GO AND CAPSIZE NOW!

WINDSURFING

CAN YOU KEEP YOUR BALANCE?

PICNICKING

BACK THIS YEAR BY POPULAR DEMAND! A SPECIAL PRIZE FOR THE MOST ORIGINAL SANDWICH. LAST YEAR'S WINNER: PIRANHA, MAYONNAISE + WATERCRESS

## Are you brave enough to ride the rapids?

If it's a really raging good time you're after, why not try your luck at white-water rafting? Feeling daring? You'll need to be. White-water rafting means hurtling over obstacles like rock-hard boulders and raging rapids . . . in a blow-up boat! Having second thoughts? What about taking Travis along to show you how it's done?

*What you need:*

- a raging river
- a really tough inflatable (blow up) raft
- a paddle (single-bladed)
- a life-jacket
- a wetsuit and a crash helmet
- five other victims (sorry, volunteers) to go with you

*What you do:*

1 Blow up your raft by the riverbank.

2 Get into the raft. Three of you should sit on each side of the raft, right up on the sides, with Travis at the back. He's in charge of steering and shouting orders!

**3** Paddle gently out into the middle of the river, then paddle straight ahead. Try to keep in time and get a nice rhythm going.

**4** Rapids ahead! You need to aim for the spot with the fewest rocks. You don't want to get a puncture. If it's in the centre, Travis will tell you to keep going straight. To turn the raft to the right, keep paddling if you're on the left. To turn left, paddle if you're on the right. (Note: to brake, you all need to paddle backwards!)

**5** Just before you hit the rapids, jump down into the bottom of the raft so you're not swept overboard as you bump over them. And prepare to get wet, soaking wet.

**6** When (hopefully) you come out on the other side, steer the raft back to the riverbank and get out. Or, if you're feeling brave, stay in the boat and keep going to the next set of rapids. . .

*A few more horribly helpful hints and tips:*
Travis thinks he's a bit of an expert when it comes to white-water rafting, so let's see how he does – and no laughing!

• Pick your rapids carefully. They're graded on a scale of 1 to 6. Grade 6 rapids are described as "nearly impossible and very dangerous, for experts only". They're wild.

Maybe start off more gently with a Grade 2...

...or a Grade 3.

THAT'S RAPIDS WITH HIGH WAVES CAPABLE OF SWAMPING AN OPEN RAFT. AAAARGHHH!

• Better still, go as part of a group and take an expert with you. They'll help you out if you run into trouble. If they don't run into trouble first. . .

• If you do fall in, try to swim down to the bottom of the rapids where the water's calmer. Then swim to the bank and get out. And whatever you do, keep hold of your paddle. Or you'll be well and truly up a creek without a paddle. . .

Don't worry if white-water rafting isn't for you. You're in good company. Sometimes even the experts get more than they'd banked on. Maybe you'd rather relax on the riverbank and read about ways of getting downriver without getting wet instead? And get to meet some real-life river rovers on the way.

# RAGING RIVER ROVING

For centuries, people have used rivers to get from A to B. Forget boring cars, trains and planes. If you wanted to visit your auntie in the next town, it was quickest to go by river. Today, rivers are still used for moving people and goods about. But in many parts of the world, cars, trains and planes have well and truly taken over.

But raging river roving didn't always have an end in sight. Sometimes intrepid explorers set off up rivers without knowing where on Earth they were going. Often they hadn't a clue what lay around the next bend in the river, let alone how they'd make it home. Sometimes it was just as well not to know. So why on Earth did they do it? Sometimes they were promised a reward. But more often than not, it was simply for the sake of having an earth-shattering adventure.

## Travels up the Niger
In the eighteenth century, some of London's leading horrible geographers set up an association for the study of African rivers.

I PROPOSE WE EXPLORE...HERE!

But it wasn't just geographical discovery they had in mind. They wanted to find a trade route into Africa and make some serious money. They desperately needed someone to go and explore the River Niger (everyone else they'd sent had died or disappeared). And in 1795, they found the perfect volunteer – a keen, young Scottish doctor called Mungo Park (1771-1806). His mission was to track the river along its entire length from source to mouth. But first he had to find it. And that was easier said than done. Over the page is how Mungo might have described his journey in his letters to his boss, Henry Beaufoy. . .

## Raging river fact file

NAME: River Niger

LOCATION: West Africa

LENGTH: 4,200 km

SOURCE: A deep ravine in the Fouta Djallon Highlands, Guinea

DRAINS: 188,340,000 sq km

MOUTH: Flows into the sea at the Gulf of Guinea in Nigeria.

FLOW FACTS:

• It's the third longest river in Africa, after the Nile and the Congo.

• Stocks of oil and gas have been found at its delta.

• The Niger's name comes from the African word 'n'ger-n-gereo' which means great river.

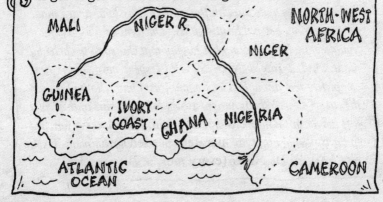

*A village in Africa, 30 March 1796*

*Dear Mr Beaufoy,*

*Thank you for your letter and the pay rise (yippee!). Fifteen shillings a day is really most generous. And it's come in the nick of time (but more of that later).*

*I don't know where on earth to begin to tell you all my news. The journey from England was most pleasant. The ship was adequate, the weather fair and the crossing took just 30 days. On landing in Africa, I headed down the River Gambia, according to plan, then continued by horse overland. (I must say, I am still rather saddlesore.)*

*For days we rode through flat, rolling grassland which made me pine for my beloved Scottish hills. The weather was also most troublesome. I was boiling hot by day and chilled to the bone by night. And it rained NON-STOP. I spent most of the time completely wet through. You see, my trusty umbrella had caught the eye of a local chieftain and I was forced to part with it as a gift (he wasn't a man to say no to). Still, I was looking forward to the challenges that lay ahead and to reaching my goal. Then, on Christmas Day, things took a turn for the worse.*

A murderous mob of bandits attacked us and stole almost everything we owned. Right down to my waistcoat buttons! And in broad daylight! Then, to cap it all, I was arrested as a spy. Me! I've never spied on anyone in my life. I tried to talk my way out of it (you know how I pride myself on talking things through) but I ended up being clapped in the local prison.

Well, I somehow managed to give the guards the slip and make my escape but by now I had nothing but the clothes I stood up in. I was in very dire straits indeed. I don't know what would have become of me if a kindly old woman hadn't given me food though she hardly had enough for herself. (So you see, the pay rise really will come in handy.)

Luckily, the robbers didn't get their thieving fingers on my precious papers which I always keep safely tucked under my hat. You'll be pleased to hear that I've taken a great many notes about local customs (with a special chapter on prisons) which I look forward to showing you on my return. If I ever return. . . Until then, I shall press on with my quest.

Yours sincerely,
Mungo Park

*Segon, on the Niger, Mali, 20 July 1796*

*Dear Mr Beaufoy,*
 *We've found it! We've found it! And it flows eastwards, not westwards as everyone thought. How it lifted my spirits to see it glistening there in the morning sun like the good old Thames at Westminster. . . It's BRILLIANT! I'm sooo excited. Yippeee!*

 *Bye for now,*
 *Mungo Park*
*PS Erm, sorry. I got a bit carried away. Very embarrassing and unscientific of me. I can promise you it won't happen again.*

---

*Somewhere up the Niger, 30 July 1796*

*Dear Mr Beaufoy,*
 *That's it – I've had it. I can't carry on. I'm tired, wet, penniless and my poor old horse is a gibbering wreck.*
 *I tried, I really tried. But enough is enough. You see, I hadn't the money for a canoe (I was robbed again – bang goes my pay rise) so, more dead than alive, my horse and I set off upstream to find the river's mouth. But it's been ten days now, and there's no end in sight. I asked a local chap if he knew where the river flowed to. He replied rather gloomily, "To the ends of the Earth." I can well believe it.*

 *Yours dejectedly, Mungo Park*

Exhausted, broke and bitterly disappointed, Mungo Park went home. He still had nightmares about prisons but things very quickly looked up. He wrote a best-selling book of his travels and became a household name. (Well, would you forget a name like Mungo?) And while he was back home, he met and married the lovely Alison and settled down in Scotland to live happily ever after. Actually it was only for a little while. Despite everything, Mungo couldn't get Africa out of his mind. When he was offered another nose at the Niger, he was off like a shot. But he still found time to write to his wife. . .

*Somewhere in West Africa, 13 June 1805*

*My Dearest Allie,*

*Half way through our journey now and things are going OK-ish, I suppose. Who am I kidding? It's been a disaster. Talk about leaving things to the last minute. It's been one delay after the other. First the soldiers sent to accompany me didn't show up (and when they did, they were a horribly bad-tempered, rowdy lot), then the supplies went missing.*

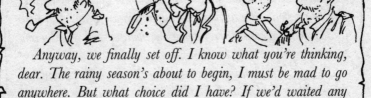

*Anyway, we finally set off. I know what you're thinking, dear. The rainy season's about to begin, I must be mad to go anywhere. But what choice did I have? If we'd waited any longer, we'd never have gone at all. And the sooner we get there, the sooner we can all go home. . .*

*Missing you dreadfully. Please don't worry. I'll be fine.*

*Your devoted Mungo*

*Sansanding, on the Niger, 17 November 1805*

*My dearest Allie,*

*We finally reached the Niger on 19 August. I'm sorry I didn't write sooner but I've been rather busy with other things. To tell you the truth, things have been going from bad to worse. The rains made the going very soggy and slow (I know, you told me so) and very few of the men made it. I suppose a more sensible chap would have given up and gone home by now. But you know me, dear. Once I make up my mind to do something, I like to see it through to the bitter end. Call me a stubborn old fool, if you like.*

*Things looked up a bit when the local chieftain promised me a couple of canoes. But they turned out to be rotten and full of holes.*

*I saved what I could of the good wood and patched it together to make a boat. It's a bit leaky but it'll have to do. And now we're heading downstream. So you see, dear, the end is really and truly in sight.*

*Dearest, I'm sending this letter by courier which should be quicker than boat. But I should be home long before it reaches you.*

*Wish you were here, or I was there.*

*All my love,*
*Your Mungo*

## A watery end

If you only like stories with a happy ending, skip the next bit. This was Mungo's last letter to his wife. He was never heard from again. Only his local guide was left to fill in the gaps. According to him, Mungo sailed 2,400 kilometres down-river, fighting off enemy canoes and nosy hippos. Another 960 kilometres and he'd have reached the river's mouth and his journey's end. Then disaster struck. Mungo was ambushed by unfriendly locals. The game was up. Rather than wait to be killed, Mungo jumped into the river and was swept away.

Did he drown? Most people think so. But not everyone. For years, rumours reached Britain of a tall, red-headed man, speaking English, and living by the Niger. . .

As for the Africa Association who got poor Mungo into this mess in the first place, they were taken over by the British government. But this didn't stop them. They sent several more expeditions to follow in Mungo Park's footsteps. In 1830, the two Clapperton brothers set off up the Niger. People sniggered because of the way they dressed, in scarlet tunics, huge baggy trousers and enormous straw hats the size of umbrellas, but the Clappertons had the last laugh. Despite their critics, they managed to sail right down the river, right to its mouth and so finally put the River Niger well and truly on the map (though they only got a £100 reward for their pains).

## River diseases

### 1 Malaria

**Symptoms:** Raging fever with a horribly high temperature. Terrible headaches, sweating and death. Especially bad in hot, swampy places.

**Cause:** Malarial mosquitoes which lay their eggs on the surface of slow-flowing rivers or ponds. When they hatch, they hover near the water. When they're hungry, they bite you, suck your blood and squirt deadly parasites into your veins. A parasite is a blood-thirsty creature that lives off other creatures. Nasty.

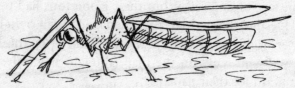

120

**Any known cure?** A course of pills usually does the trick. And of course it helps if you don't get bitten in the first place. Use mosquito repellant, cover up (particularly at dusk) and sleep under a mosquito net. An old-fashioned explorer's cure is to slap mud on your face! Well, it should take your mind off things!

## 2 River blindness

**Symptoms:** Horribly itchy skin. Damaged eyesight and in the worst cases blindness.

**Cause:** Blackflies which live and breed in tropical rivers. They bite you and spit tiny grubs into the wound.

Inside you, these grow into worms and lay their eggs which hatch into millions more worms. The worms spread through your body. Dead worms inside your eyes can make you go blind. Horrible.

**Any known cure?** A yearly dose of medicine, taken by mouth, can prevent blindness. Spraying rivers where blackflies breed helps to keep the disease at bay.

### 3 Bilharzia (bill-har-zi-a)

**Symptoms:** Itchy skin or rash, fever, chills, aches, pains and death. Can seriously damage your liver, guts, kidneys and bladder. So nothing too serious, then!

**Cause:** Tiny worm grubs. They live inside tropical river snails.

Then the grubs swap the snails for you. If you're in the river at the same time, the grubs can burrow through your skin and into your blood. There they lay their eggs. Yuk!

**Any known cure?** Yes, a simple injection or a course of pills.

### Could you be a river rover?

Could you follow in Mungo Park's footsteps and become a raging river rover? Picture the scene... You've been walking for miles. You're tired, your feet hurt, you've been munched by what feels like a million mosquitoes and you just want to go home. You can see the path you need to take but, guess what? It's on the other side of a raging river!

So how on Earth do you get across? Decide which one of these methods you think would work best? Then check out the answers on pages 126–130.

1 Take a boat across it. Obvious really, but the question is what sort of boat do you choose? Take your pick from these raging river rovers.

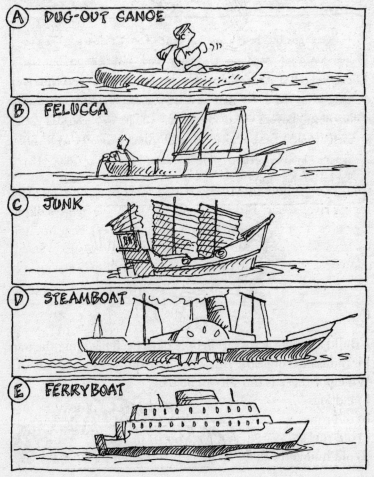

(A) DUG-OUT CANOE

(B) FELUCCA

(C) JUNK

(D) STEAMBOAT

(E) FERRYBOAT

## F CRUISESHIP

If you go by boat, watch out for sandbars. They're big dunes of sand on the river bed, ruffled up by the current. And they're horribly hazardous. The problem is they're so hard to spot and can suddenly shift without warning. Before you know it, you'll be grounded or even sunk. Best take a pilot with you (that's an expert in navigation). He'll know the river like the back of his hand.

**2** Build a bridge across it. People have been bridging the gap for thousands of years. But what have bridges been made of? Which of these is too silly to be true?

a) old logs
b) old ropes
c) old rocks
d) old human heads

**3** Dig a tunnel under it. Go on, get shovelling. It's not as silly as it sounds. There are several tunnels running under the River Thames in England. The first was built to last in 1842 by British engineer Marc Brunel. It was the first underwater tunnel in history. Today tube trains race through it.

**4** Swim across it. If you're a strong swimmer, take a good, deep breath and dive in. But if your doggy paddle lets you down, you might need some help. If you can't be seen dead in armbands, hold on to a floating log for support. Or do what the ancient Assyrians did and grab on to a blown-up pig's bladder instead! Before you jump in, slap on plenty of insect repellant!

**5** Pole vault over it. If all else fails, you could always go and take a running jump. . .

**Answers:**

**1** All these boats can be used on rivers but it depends which river you choose. For fast-flowing rivers, dug-out canoes are just the job. They're light, tough and easy to steer. But watch out for particularly strong currents. Before you know it, you'll be swept downstream. To get over the river, paddle across and slightly upstream, HARD! For busy rivers, feluccas are neat and nippy for weaving in and out of traffic. They've been used on the Nile since Ancient Egyptian times. For deep, wide rivers, why not jump on a Chinese junk. Hope you're feeling strong. If the river's too high or too low, you might have to get out and pull. But if raging river currents are a problem, you'll need a boat with an engine. You could go for a modern motorboat but a classic old steamboat would really impress your friends. They were once a frequent sight on the Mississippi but now they mostly take tourists around. Fancy a bet? Some steamboats double up as floating casinos. For very wide rivers, hop on the ferry. Most big rivers have one. But get there early. They're often the only lift around and they can get horribly crowded. And finally, for rivers with history on their side, a cruiseship's the perfect choice. If you're feeling flash, why not cruise along the River Nile. You can see all the sights without leaving your deckchair.

**2 d)** Of course, you don't actually get bridges *built* of heads! Most of old London Bridge across the River Thames was made of sensible stone. But it also had a row of sharp spikes at each end. And guess what was on the ends of the spikes – yes, the chopped-off heads of traitors and criminals! Gruesome!

The very first bridges were probably logs or stepping stones laid across a stream. Rope bridges are often used in the jungle, made from vines. You have to hold on tight, as they wobble a lot.

Yes, bridges are often the quickest and easiest way of crossing a river. But you'll need to choose the right type. Are you brave enough to find out how to build a bridge?

*What you need:*
- some logs (assorted lengths)
- some stones
- a raging river

*What you do:*

**a)** Lay a long log across the river so it reaches from one bank to the other. Congratulations! You've made a simple beam bridge and it's great for crossing a narrow river.

GOOD DOG... GO AND FETCH THE FIRE BRIGADE...

**b)** For a wider river, you'll need a longer log and it needs to be stronger. Otherwise it will sag in the middle as you walk across it.

**c)** On a very wide river, you'll need to lay several logs end to end. Put a few piles of stones in the water for the logs to rest on. Technically, these piles are called piers.

RIVER

BEAM OF LOGS

PIERS: TOPS STICK JUST ABOVE THE WATER

Note: if the river's horribly deep and wide, forget beam bridges. The logs and piers would be just too huge. Instead you'll need a suspension bridge. That's a bridge which hangs from long, steel cables suspended from tall towers. These bridges can be more than a kilometre long. And that's a job for a proper engineer!

*Horrible Health Warning*
*Messing about on rivers can be dangerous. Be careful that you don't slip and fall in. The water may be deeper than you think and there may be strong currents which could sweep you away.*

**3** Tunnelling can work but be careful. Even for experts, underwater tunnels are tricky to build. Because they go under the soft riverbed rocks, their roofs and walls can easily cave in. Brunel had to design a special tunnelling machine for the job. It burrowed through the rock, holding up the roof while the workers were left to line the tunnel. Clever, eh? Especially when you know that Brunel got the idea from watching a wood-boring mollusc at work. Modern tunnelling machines are still based on Brunel's brilliant invention.

**4** This is a good idea, if you can swim, though maybe leave out the pig. And watch out for weirs. They're small, low dams built across the river and they block the river to make a deep pool like a small harbour for boats. They're often hidden by the water – making them doubly dangerous. If you're swept over one, you'll get sucked into the swirling water and you won't be able to get out again. They're just as dangerous if you're in a small boat.

**5** Strangely enough, you'd be in good company. Believe it or not but this is how the sport of pole vaulting began with people using sticks to leap across streams. You should easily make it if the river's narrow but get a good run up if it's wide. Otherwise you're in for a horribly soggy landing.

So, which works best? Well, there's no real right or wrong answer to that because all raging rivers are different!

*Earth-shattering fact*
*What if the river's too narrow or shallow to take big ships? You make it deeper and wider, of course! That's what engineers did to the St Lawrence River in North America. And they tacked some canals on the end. Ships can now make the 3769-kilometre trip from the Atlantic Ocean and across the Great Lakes in just eight days. The only snag is that the waterway's blocked by ice in winter and there's nothing the engineers can do about that!*

You might think that deadly diseases, life-threatening weirs and leaky canoes were the worst that the river could throw at you. But you'd be wrong, horribly wrong. So far, your river's been quite well behaved. It's true. But things are about to change. Prepare to be swept off your feet. You're about to see the other side of the river. A side you haven't seen before. When the river's true colours come flooding out. . .

If you think things look bad when your teacher loses his temper, beware of a river in a rage. In a flash, a river can change completely from a nice, babbling brook to a raging torrent. If this happens to a river near you, get out of the way, fast! Furious floods can be horribly hazardous, sweeping away everything in their path. INCLUDING YOU! And the freaky thing is that they can happen anywhere, anytime. . .

## What on Earth is a flood?

Want to find out about floods but too wet to ask? Worried about keeping your head above water? Here's Travis to throw you in at the deep end. . .

> SO, WHAT ON EARTH IS A FLOOD THEN ?

It's when a raging river overflows because it's too full of water. Simple really. Like when you fill a glass too full of pop.

> HMM, I SEE, AND WHY DOES THIS HAPPEN ?

Most floods happen when massive, and I mean massive, amounts of rain fall in a very short time. The river just can't cope. You also get floods when melting snow swells the river or when a dodgy dam bursts. Or when cyclones or tidal waves whip up the sea into a frenzy.

> BLIMEY! WHERE DOES ALL THE OVERFLOW GO ?

It spills on to the floodplain. That's the flat land on either side of the river which is normally dry. It can be a few metres across or a few hundred kilometres, and it's made of mud and sand dumped by the river.

WHY DOESN'T THE WATER JUST SOAK INTO THE GROUND? THEN IT WOULDN'T MATTER IF THE RIVER FLOODED.

Good point. But it's not as simple as that, I'm sorry to say. If the rain's very heavy, the ground can't soak it up fast enough and the soil becomes water-logged. Then any floodwater just lies on top.

AND ARE FLOODS REALLY DANGEROUS?

Yes and no. Some rivers flood every year without doing much damage. But a really fierce flood can be fatal. It can drown fields and crops, wash away buildings and cause millions of pounds of damage. And cost lives. In fact, furious floods do more damage and kill more people than any other natural disaster. And that's official! The worst flood on record happened in 1931, when the Huang He River in China burst its banks killing no less than 4 million people and leaving 80 million homeless. Horrible.

WHY DON'T PEOPLE LIVE SOMEWHERE SAFER?

Millions of people don't have much choice. They live in countries where there's already too little land to go round. Besides, the soil on the floodplain is so fantastically fertile, they're willing to run the risk.

Most rivers can turn nasty if conditions are right. But without doubt one of riskiest is the raging Yangtze River in China. . .

# The Daily Globe

## Sunday 2 August 1998, Hunan Province, eastern China

# MILLIONS IN FEAR AS FLOOD WATERS RISE

A week after the Yangtze burst its banks for the third time in two months, millions of Chinese are still on full flood alert. Today, water levels on the river broke all previous records, leaving terrified villagers in fear of being literally washed away.

The Yangtze has been rising since spring, placing enormous pressure on the fragile system of dykes or embankments which separate the river from the 200 million people living along its banks. With floodwater now surging downstream, people are getting really very frightened.

"We're praying we can prevent a disaster," an elderly villager told our reporter. "We've been making the dykes round our village higher with mud. But if the dykes don't hold when the river comes, we'll lose everything."

DAM BUILDERS

Elsewhere in the region some dykes have already collapsed and several villages lie swamped under two metres of water. This year's floods have already claimed 2,500 lives – numbers are still rising – and driven millions of villagers out of their homes. Some have been stranded for days on their roofs, helplessly watching the unstoppable rise of the water.

ROOF TOPS

And now a new danger is lurking. Doctors are warning that disease could be the next disaster to strike. In some places, polluted floodwater has already contaminated drinking water and placed millions at risk of sickness and diarrhoea.

But getting the sick to hospital is no easy matter.

"I saw some people being rowed to hospital in boats," an eyewitness said. "But the first floor of the hospital was under water. I don't know how they got in."

So, who is to blame for the disaster? This is a question many people are asking. True, the river has been flooding for centuries but this year's torrential summer rains have made the problem much worse. Some people blame the government for not spending enough money on repairing the dykes. If they don't act soon, locals fear, the same thing will happen again and again.

"I have nothing," one farmer told us after he'd seen his home, all his belongings and his crops completely washed away. "I'll have to start all over again."

And this may not be the last time. . .

# Raging river fact file

NAME: Yangtze River

LOCATION: China

LENGTH: 6,418 km

SOURCE: Mount Gelandandong, Tibet

DRAINS: 1,683,500 sq km

MOUTH: Flows into the East China Sea (part of the Pacific Ocean) near Shanghai.

FLOW FACTS:

• In Chinese, it's called the Chang Jiang or Long River. Legend says it was carved out by a goddess.

• It's the world's third longest river after the Nile and Amazon.

• About three-quarters of all the rice grown in China is grown on its floodplain.

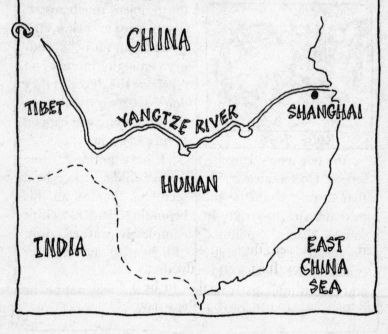

*The 1998 Yangtze flood was what horrible geographers call a 100-year flood. But what on Earth does this mean? Well, floods are rated by how often they might happen. The more frequent they are, the better. A one-year flood is likely to happen once a year and doesn't do much damage. A 100-year flood means that, each year, there's a one-in-a-hundred chance of a flood that can do a lot of damage. Making it horribly dangerous. Phew! If that sounds bad, imagine the horror of the people of Lynmouth, England, when a freak 50,000-year flood smashed their village to pieces in 1952.*

*At least there shouldn't be another flood like it (with that river, at any rate!) for a very, very long time.*

## Could you be a flood hydrologist?

Once a river's in full flood, there's nothing scientists can do to stop it. But they can try to find out where a flood will strike next. If they can work out when and where a flood's likely to happen, they can sound the alarm and get people out of the way. It isn't easy – floods are horribly fickle.

Do you have what it takes to be a flood hydrologist? (That's the posh title for a horrible scientist who studies floods.)

# HORRIBLE JOB ADVERT

Tired of keeping your feet on the ground?
Is life driving you round the bend? Fancy
a spell in the fast stream? Why not join
our team of top hydrologists?
- You must like the outdoors and be a
strong swimmer.

- You must be good at maths and making
graphs (especially flow charts).

- You mustn't mind getting your feet wet.

- Full training will be given.
Still interested? Why not meander along
to your local Careers Centre?

**Raging rivers – the career you can bank on.**

And here's Travis to show you the ropes. . .

**Travis's (almost) fool-proof guide to flood forecasting**
**1 Get to know your river**
You need to study your river carefully and get to know all of its twists and turns. Most importantly, you need to see how it reacts when it rains. Ask yourself these two questions:
**a)** How much rain is falling? You don't need loads of posh measuring gear for this. You can make a simple rain gauge from a kitchen measuring jug.

But serious scientists also scan the skies for rain using high-tech radars and weather satellites.
**b)** How much is the river rising? Scientists study river levels with a nifty gadget called a stream sensor. It radios back data to a computer.
**c)** Some hot-shot hydrologists go a step further and build their own model river, complete with fake meanders, floodplains and floods. They use this to test how the river reacts and how dams and dykes hold up against floods.

FLASH FLOOD!

## 2 Chart your river's progress

Next, feed all your info into a computer. It will do loads of earth-shattering equations and plot the results on a chart. (The posh name for this is a hydrograph.) (But you'll need to double check it's got things right and that's where being wicked at maths will help.) The chart will show how the river copes with rain, and how long before it overflows. From this you can work out how likely a flood is, and how long you've got to get outta there. . .

## 3 Sound the alarm

If it's raining heavily and the river's rising rapidly, for goodness' sake sound the alarm! In Britain, flood warnings are colour-coded according to the degree of risk.

- **Yellow Warning**

  Risk of flooding to low-lying farmland and roads near rivers.

- **Amber Warning**

  Risk of flooding to isolated homes and larger areas of farmland near rivers.

- **Red Warning**

  Risk of serious flooding to many properties, roads and large areas of farmland.

So how watertight was your warning? Of course, you can't tell for sure until the flood's been and gone. The trouble is that floods are horribly unpredictable. You can't always work out what they'll do next. For big rivers like the Mississippi, you might have a week's warning of flooding. But you might have just a few hours to flee from a flash flood. (That's a flood that rises incredibly quickly after an unusually heavy downpour of rain.)

## Stopping the flow

You know the saying, "Prevention is better than cure"? It means that it's better to stop your teeth rotting in the first place by not eating too many sweets than to spend hours afterwards at the dentist. It's usually used about people. But the same could be said for floods. You might not be able to stop a flood in mid-flow but you can take steps to reduce the damage. How? Well, for a start, you could. . .

- **Plant some trees.** Here's how it works:

**1** Plant leaves trap rain before it can hit the ground. In a forest, about three-quarters of rain is waylaid like this.

**2** Plant roots suck up water from the soil, and also bind the soil together.

The problem is that plants and trees are being cut down for firewood or to clear farmland. And this means there's nothing to stop the rain pouring into the river. The rain also washes away loads of loose soil which raises the river bed so it floods more easily.

- **Change the shape of the river.** Try making the river straighter, wider and deeper. It'll work wonders. It makes it easier for the river to flow so it reaches the sea faster without overflowing. But you'll need a special digging machine called a dredger.

- **Change the river's course.** By building a ditch or channel to divert the water away. It's also useful for storing spare water. These diverting ditches are called spillways.

- **Dam it.** Dams are horribly handy for flood control. But are they any good? Who better to ask than a couple of horrible hydrologists? The only problem is finding two hydrologists that agree. About anything! Take these two, for a start:

DAMS ARE BRILLIANT BECAUSE THEY STOP RIVERS FLOODING, AND WE KNOW HOW USEFUL THAT IS. AND THEY MAKE SURE THERE'S A STEADY SUPPLY OF WATER FOR DRINKING AND FARMING. AND THEY CAN GENERATE LOADS OF CHEAP CLEAN ELECTRICITY. WHAT MORE COULD YOU ASK?

DAMS ARE DISASTROUS BECAUSE THEY FORCE MILLIONS OF PEOPLE OUT OF THEIR HOUSES AND DROWN THE LAND UNDER TONNES OF WATER. THEY ALSO WIPE OUT WILDLIFE. AND IF YOU WAVE GOODBYE TO FLOODS, IT'S BYE BYE FERTILE FLOOD-PLAINS AND DELTAS TOO. BESIDES DAMS COST A FORTUNE TO BUILD AND WHAT HAPPENS IF ONE GOES AND BURSTS?

Talk about putting a spanner in the works! It's difficult to know just who to believe.

• **Build an embankment.** One of the oldest ways to stop a flood is to make the riverbank higher. You could do this by building a mud or concrete embankment, or dyke. But does this waterproofing work? The answer is, Sometimes it does, and sometimes it doesn't. Along the Mississippi, embankments are called levees. (That's French for "raised".) There are thousands of kilometres of them along the river. For years, they've been the main flood-proofing measure. But what happens when a levee springs a leak? Then things go horribly wrong, as the terrible true story on the next page shows. . .

## Raging river fact file

NAME: Mississippi River

LOCATION: USA

LENGTH: 3,780 km

SOURCE: Lake Itasca, Minnesota, USA

DRAINS: 3,256,000 sq km

MOUTH: Flows into the Gulf of Mexico (part of the Atlantic Ocean) at its huge delta.

FLOW FACTS:

• Its longest tributary, the Missouri, is actually 350 km longer than the Mississippi itself. The two rivers meet near St Louis.

• New Orleans is protected by several long levees. Which is just as well because the city lies below river level!

• Its nicknames include Old Man River and Big Muddy.

WHAT THEY SAID ABOUT IT: "You cannot tame that lawless stream." (Mark Twain)

# After the Great Flood, summer 1993

For millions of people living along the Mississippi floods are a fact of life. But things seemed to be getting better. It had been 20 years since the last big flood and, with higher and stronger levees, backed up by new dams and spillways, floods seemed a thing of the past.

The new measures seemed to have done the trick. Or had they? True, it had been a very wet year with record-breaking rains. But the floods, if they came, usually happened in spring. By summer, the river was usually falling. What happened that summer took everyone by surprise.

With no break in the rain, the Mississippi became a raging torrent, flowing at six times its usual speed. In places, it rose seven metres above normal, a raging brown torrent of water and mud.

The new flood measures failed miserably. In the state of Illinois alone, 17 levees crumbled under the strain . . . including the one protecting the little town of Valmeyer.

Local people worked round the clock, filling thousands of sandbags to fight back the flow. But despite their best efforts, they could not stop the wall of water which poured into the town.

Fortunately, the town had just been evacuated. Miraculously, only one person died and no one was seriously injured. Everyone knew that it could have been much worse.

Three weeks later, the townspeople were allowed to return home to start the massive clean-up. Valmeyer had been turned into a waterlogged ghost town. Windows were smashed, all the lights were out, and thick muddy sludge covered everything. The eerie quietness was broken only by the buzzing of huge swarms of mosquitoes.

"It's heartbreaking," one man said as he looked at the wreckage of his home. "I've lived here all my life and it's all gone. Everything's covered in mud and mould. But at least we've got each other and a disaster sure makes folk rally round." Only four houses were left standing. Others were water-filled wrecks. Their only occupants were frogs, crayfish and . . . poisonous snakes. Everyone had to up sticks and start all over again. (And after a second soaking in September, that's exactly what happened. The whole town moved lock, stock and barrel, to higher, drier ground.)

The Great Flood of 1993 was America's worst natural disaster. The flood covered an area the size of England and seven states were declared disaster zones. The water caused $10 billion of damage, flooded 50 towns, destroyed 43,000 homes and left 70,000 people homeless. Millions of acres of crops were washed away. And only a quarter of the levees were left in one piece.

*Earth-shattering fact*
*Imagine a busy city like London. Now imagine it under a metre of water. . . All it would take is a high tide surging up the River Thames from the sea. To stop such a disaster, a massive barrier was built across the Thames in 1984. When high tides are due, ten huge steel gates swing up from the river bed to make a gigantic dam. The barrier's already had to close more than 30 times. . .*

# Travis's top waterproof flood warnings

If building a dam is beyond you, or your homework doesn't leave you enough time, what on Earth can you do if a flood's flowing your way? Try to remember these basic Do's and Don'ts and you'll save yourself from a soaking:

**DO...**

• Stay tuned to your radio for flood warnings.

Or listen out for a siren, if time's short. Some countries run a telephone flood-warning service. If you can get to the phone...

• Switch off the gas and electricity. Water and electricity are an explosive mix. NEVER touch electrical equipment with wet hands. Ever. Water is a brilliant conductor of electricity which means that electricity can shoot through it very easily indeed. And it could give you a killer shock.

• Stock up on sandbags. If you're staying put, block up doorways and air bricks with sandbags. You can buy them or make your own from some strong cloth sacks and sand.

• Go upstairs. And take any other people, pets and valuables with you, out of reach of the water.

• Pack some supplies. Whether you're going or staying, you'll need emergency stores to tide you over for a few days. Pack warm clothes, blankets, food, water, a torch and some batteries. Stuff these in strong plastic bags ready to grab when you need them.
• Be prepared to leave home. If the flood's really serious, you may have to move fast. Head for higher ground away from the river. Better still, go to stay with some friends.

Once you're outside. . .
**DON'T**. . .
• Try to cross any floodwater by foot. If it reaches your ankles, turn back and find another route. The water may be deeper than it looks and the road underneath may have been washed away.

• Go for a drive. At least, not through flood water. It often flows fast enough to wash cars away. And cars can quickly turn into death-traps if you break down. By the time the water reaches the windows, the water pressure will be too strong for you to open the door. If you do have to drive, open the windows before you set off. That'll equalize the pressure inside and outside the car.

• Drink any floodwater. However thirsty you are. Floodwater's filthy, thanks to all the mud, debris and even sewage it sucks along. Ideal for germs to fester in. If you're staying at home, fill the bath with clean water, and boil any water you use.

• Camp near a river bed. Even if it looks dry. It could fill up in seconds and wash you away.

• Ever try to outrun the flood. However fast you run, it'll be right behind you. . .

You might think that spending your whole life studying water might turn a hydrologist's brain horribly soggy and soft. But these soaking scientists are not as wet as they seem.

They're working their socks off trying to forecast floods more accurately. The good news is that they're getting quicker at spotting the warning signs and moving people out of the way. The bad news is that forecasts can never be watertight. It can't be a cut and dried case. Why? Well, floods are just too horribly unpredictable.

# REVOLTING RIVERS

Never mind messing about on rivers. After everything rivers have done for us, what are we doing in return? The sickening answer is making a mess of them. Horrible humans have made some rivers so disgustingly dirty, they've been declared officially DEAD! (The revolting rivers, not the humans. Though if your drinking water came from one of them, you might soon be a gonner too.) So why on Earth is freshwater so filthy? Why not. . .

## Make you own rancid river soup

*What you need:*

- stinking sewage (it's usually treated in a sewage works before it's clean enough to be pumped into the river but in some places it goes in . . . as it is!)
- filthy factory waste (this might be dirty water or poisonous metals and chemicals)
- fertilizers and pesticides (washed off farmers' fields)

*What you do:*

1 Chuck all the ingredients into a river and leave to fester.

2 Sprinkle a few bottles and tin cans on top.

3 Now offer a bowlful to your teacher!

# Raging river fact file

NAME: River Ganges
LOCATION: India and Bangladesh
LENGTH: 2,510 km
SOURCE: Gangotri glacier, Himalayas
MOUTH: Flows into the Indian Ocean at the Bay of Bengal.
DRAINS: 975,900 sq km
FLOW FACTS:

- It joins the Brahmaputra River in Bangladesh and empties into the world's biggest delta.
- A huge mangrove swamp stretches along the delta. It's home to man-eating crocodiles and tigers.
- About half a billion people live on its floodplain.

## Cleaning up the gungy Ganges

For millions of people living along the Ganges, the river doubles up as a water supply and a drain. They don't have the money for posh treatment plants, so every day, millions of litres of smelly sewage and killer chemicals are flushed straight into the river. And that's not all. . .

Many people believe that the river is holy and that bathing in its water will wash their sins away. People also come to the river to die. Their bodies are cremated (burnt), then their ashes are thrown into the water. Sometimes bodies are also thrown in. Animal and human bodies. It may sound morbid to you but for people in India it's very important. The problem is that it's not doing the river much good. Some of the Ganges is so horribly polluted that it's putting people's health at risk.

In 1985 things got so bad that a massive clean-up campaign began. Part of the plan was to build hundreds of new sewage treatment works. (Warning – you'll need a strong stomach for the next bit.) Another part of the plan was to flood the river with turtles. Yes, turtles. Meat-eating turtles who would munch up the dead. Gruesome but brilliant.

But has it worked? Is the gungy Ganges now gleaming with health? Well, not exactly; but it's certainly getting cleaner – though how much of that is down to the tasteless turtles, no one can really tell.

*Earth-shattering fact*
*In 1858, the smell from the River Thames was so bad that it put MPs (Members of Parliament) in the nearby Houses of Parliament right off their work. They renamed the river the Great Stink. Thank goodness things have got a bit more fragrant.*

## Fragrant flowers

But it isn't all doom and gloom. The good news is that people are really trying to clean up their act. On many rivers, action plans are already up and running. Remember the reeking Rhine? For years it was known as the 'sewer of Europe'. Well, things are now looking up. The river was well-stocked with salmon until about 50 years ago. (Salmon are particularly sensitive to pollution.) The aim is to bring the salmon swimming back in the next few years. And there are strict rules to help it happen.

Which is great news for raging rivers all over the world. And for you. Before very long, you'll be back by the riverbank, a drink and a fishing rod in your hands, with not a horrible field trip in sight. . .

**If you're still interested in finding out more, here are some websites you can visit:**

**http://www.amrivers.org/**
North America's leading national river conservation organization

**http://www.cis.umassd.edu/~gleung/**
Yellow River, the longest river in China, has its own homepage!

**http://www.irn.org/**
International Rivers Network, working to halt destructive river development projects

**http://www.highway57.co.uk/tbvc**
Find out about the Thames Barrier, the world's largest movable flood barrier.

**http://www.nps:gov/yose/note3.htm**
A waterfall picture book from Yosemite National Park, California.

**http://www.amazonthefilm.com/**
The official Amazon river website with photos, a quiz and even an Amazon movie!

# HORRIBLE SCIENCE

**Science with the squishy bits left in!**

*Also available:*

**Blood, Bones and Body Bits**
Find out which animals live on your eyelashes.

**Ugly Bugs**
The insect world goes underneath the magnifying glass.

**Chemical Chaos**
What would make the worst stink bomb in the world ever?

**Nasty Nature**
Explore the nasty side of the animal world.

**Fatal Forces**
Find out how to sleep on a bed of nails – without becoming
a human pin cushion.

**Vicious Veg**
Ever wondered what stops trees from falling over?

**Disgusting Digestion**
Follow the incredible adventures of your own stomach.

**Sounds Dreadful**
Get the low down on why farts are so noisy.

# HORRIBLE SCIENCE

**Evolve or Die**
Dig up the dirt on survival and extinction.

**Bulging Brains**
Get your head round some amazing brain facts.

**Frightening Light**
Discover what really happens when there's an eclipse.

*Look out for:*

**Suffering Scientists Special**
Scientific geniuses as you've never seen them before!

**Science has never been so horrible!**

# 'Horrible Geography'

**Geography with the gritty bits left in!**

*Also available:*

**Violent Volcanoes**
Venture into the fiery world of volcanoes – it's an
explosive read!

**Odious Oceans**
Dive into murky waters and come face-to-face with sharks,
pirates and poisonous fish!

**Stormy Weather**
Enter the turbulent world of weather where tornadoes and
thunderstorms knock you off your feet.

**Geography has never been so horrible!**